I0393860

Table of Contents

Instructions

The Program Plan outlines pending grant funding opportunities (solicitations) that will be awarded based on Fiscal Year (FY) 2012 appropriations. It provides constituent groups a single, comprehensive guide to current funding opportunities and the latest agency initiatives.

The Program Plan describes competitive, continuation, and formula grants (see Glossary in Appendix C), opportunities for training and technical assistance, and other resources available to the justice community. Contact information is provided with each program description.

The Program Plan is organized by topic. Users can scroll through the discretionary programs, training and technical assistance, and research and statistics subsections found within each topical chapter. All programs in the Program Plan are listed alphabetically in the index in Appendix E. The Web links that are part of each program description will take the user to the OJP component page where additional details and updates can be found. Frequently Asked Questions are found in Appendix D.

Discretionary grants are generally awarded to eligible recipients at the discretion of the awarding agency. Formula grants are awarded based on a statutory formula. A list of OJP formula grants is available in Appendix B. For information about state formula grants, contact the State Administering Agency (SAA). A list of SAAs is available at www.ojp.usdoj.gov/saa/. A list of OJP continuation grants can be found in Appendix A.

An overview of the grant process, as well as the grant management and application review process, is available through the Grants 101 section of the Funding area of the OJP Web site at http://www.ojp.gov/grants101/. The materials available at this site will help grant recipients follow rules, submit required reports, and understand the grant oversight conducted by OJP to prevent fraud, waste, and abuse of taxpayer dollars. All applicants that meet grant solicitation requirements are considered equally in accordance with the process detailed at this site.

Grant solicitations are posted throughout the year and, in most cases, remain open for several weeks. Solicitations can be found at www.grants.gov, www.ojp.gov/funding/funding.htm. Grants.gov is a comprehensive source for information about competitive grants available from all federal agencies. This Web site provides grant descriptions, forms, instructions, helpful hints, and support to apply and succeed in the grant process. Applicants are encouraged to visit these sites, register using the instructions found at www.grants.gov/applicants/get_registered.jsp, and begin the grant application process early.

Information on the Grants Management System (GMS) is available at www.ojp.gov/training/gmstraining.htm. Assistance with the grant application process is available through the GMS Online Training Tool (www.ojp.usdoj.gov/gmscbt/), which provides step-by-step instructions for how to use the various modules within GMS; by e-mailing the GMS Help Desk; or by calling 202-514-2024 (option 3) for technical assistance.

Section 1

Initiatives to Address a Wide Range of Criminal and Juvenile Justice Issues

Overview

Several OJP initiatives, including many fellowships and some training and technical assistance initiatives, cover a broad range of criminal and juvenile justice issues. While many initiatives that cross-cut more than one topical issue are found throughout the Program Plan, this section includes those that touch many areas and may have no single area of emphasis.

In addition, many of the programs in this section support OJP's efforts to ensure that communities and their partners have the necessary tools to be successful, including the following:

- information about how federal funding works in their communities;
- access to a full range of technical assistance and training;
- knowledge from other communities about programs that work;
- data, research, and evaluations for use in strategic planning;
- strong public and private institutional partnerships; and
- online resources and access to technology.

Discretionary Programs

Program Name Edward Byrne Memorial Competitive Grant Program—National Initiatives
FY 2012 Funding $13,382,623
OJP Sponsor BJA
Web Link www.bja.gov
Program Contact Bureau of Justice Assistance, (202) 616-6500
Program Description
The Byrne Competitive Program helps local communities improve the capacity of state and local justice systems by providing national support efforts, including training and technical assistance strategically targeted to address local needs. Several solicitations are expected to be released under the Byrne Competitive Program that will focus on national initiatives in the areas of criminal courts, indigent defense, and justice information sharing. In addition, a solicitation will be released seeking Visiting Fellows to assist with national priority policy areas.

Eligible applicants include national, regional, state, or local public and private entities, including for-profit and nonprofit organizations, faith-based and community organizations, institutions of higher education, tribal jurisdictions, and units of local government that support national initiatives to improve the functioning of the criminal justice system. For-profit organizations must agree to waive any profit or fees for services. Joint applications are permissible, with one agency being the applicant agency.

Solicitations under this program will be released on a rolling basis, and are expected to be released from February–April, 2012. Awards under this program will be made by September 30, 2012.

Program Name Byrne Criminal Justice Innovation Initiative
FY 2012 Funding $13,472,623
OJP Sponsor BJA
Web Link www.bja.gov
Program Contact Bureau of Justice Assistance, (202) 616-6500
Program Description:
The Byrne Criminal Justice Innovation (BCJI) Initiative supports place-based, data- and research-

driven projects to build and enhance the capacity of communities to create comprehensive strategies to address priority crime problems. BCJI employs strategies to build the capacity of distressed communities to better prevent and reduce crime and enhance conditions that contribute to community crime, as well as to expand efforts of communities to more comprehensively address these crime issues. This would include continuation of the Building Neighborhood Capacity training and technical assistance effort, which builds the capacity of the most distressed communities to develop comprehensive crime strategies. In addition, BJA plans to issue a solicitation to make site-based awards to implement or enhance the BCJI model.

Program Name Coordinated Tribal Assistance Solicitation
FY 2012 Funding BJA $28,130,978; OJJDP $600,000 for Tribal Juvenile Accountability Discretionary Grants and $6,300,000 for Tribal Youth Program; OVC $3,600,000 for Tribal Victim Assistance and $2,700,000 for Children's Justice Act
OJP Sponsor BJA, OJJDP, and OVC
Web Link www.justice.gov/tribal/grants.html
Program Contact CTAS Response Center, 1-800-421-6770
Program Description:
The Department of Justice launched its Coordinated Tribal Assistance Solicitation (CTAS) in FY 2010 in direct response to concerns raised by tribal leaders about the Department's grant process that did not provide the flexibility tribes needed to address their criminal justice and public safety needs. Through CTAS, federally recognized tribes and tribal consortia are able to submit a single application for most of DOJ's tribal grant programs. DOJ designed this comprehensive approach to save time and resources and allow tribes and DOJ to gain a better understanding of the tribes' overall public safety needs. CTAS is a collaborative effort across the following DOJ components, bureaus, and offices.

- OJP's Bureau of Justice Assistance (BJA)
- Executive Office for United States Attorneys (EOUSA)
- Office of Community Policing Services (COPS)
- OJP's Office of Juvenile Justice and Delinquency Prevention (OJJDP)
- Office of Tribal Justice (OTJ)
- OJP's Office for Victims of Crime (OVC)
- Office on Violence Against Women (OVW)

Program Name Tribal Justice Capacity Building Training and Technical Assistance Program
FY 2012 Funding $4,000,000
OJP Sponsor BJA
Web Link www.bja.gov
Program Contact Julius Dupree, (202) 514-1928, julius.dupree@usdoj.gov
Program Description
This program provides training and technical assistance to tribes on a range of capacity building issues, including tribal justice system strategic planning and state/tribal justice system collaboration. Through this program, training will be made available on information sharing, best practices, and new and evidence-based models of service.

Training and Technical Assistance

Program Name State Justice Statistics Technical Assistance Program
FY 2012 Funding $650,000
OJP Sponsor BJS
Web Link bjs.ojp.usdoj.gov
Program Contact Devon B. Adams, (202) 514-9157, Devon.Adams@usdoj.gov
Program Description
BJS will seek to fund a State Justice Statistics Technical Assistance Program having four main components: Information Acquisition and Dissemination; the Technical Assistance Program; the

Incident-Based Reporting Resource Center; and the Domestic Violence and Sexual Assault Data Resource Center. The goals of the project are to enhance the technical, research, and organizational capabilities of states to collect and analyze justice statistics; foster and coordinate the exchange of information and technology among local, state, and federal agencies; facilitate and coordinate policy-oriented research in the states consistent with the themes of the BJS State Justice Statistics Program for Statistical Analysis Centers (SAC); serve as a forum for expressing the common concerns and perspectives of state analysts; establish and promote professional standards for criminal justice researchers and policy analysts; and serve as liaison among the SACs and between state statistical agencies and BJS, as well as other OJP agencies.

Research and Statistical Programs

Program Name State Justice Statistics Program for State Statistical Analysis Centers
FY 2012 Funding $2,800,000
OJP Sponsor BJS
Web Link bjs.ojp.usdoj.gov
Program Contact Devon B. Adams, (202) 514-9157, Devon.Adams@usdoj.gov
Program Description
The State Justice Statistics (SJS) Program is designed to maintain and enhance each state's capacity to address criminal justice issues through collection and analysis of data. Through the SJS Program, BJS provides limited funds to State Statistical Analysis Centers in each state to coordinate statistical activities within the state, conduct research as needed to estimate impacts of legislative and policy changes, and serve a liaison role in assisting BJS to gather data from respondent agencies within their states. The SJS Program is designed to: (a) enhance the capabilities of the states to collect, analyze, and interpret data on justice issues relevant to the states and the nation; (b) make maximum use of state statistical organizations and state-level data collected by BJS and other Department of Justice components; (c) provide a mechanism that supports the collection and sharing of vital justice system data among the states and between state and federal government; and (d) better serve the information needs of the states and federal government by providing a core body of knowledge about the administration of criminal justice in each state.

Program Name NIJ Ph.D. Graduate Research Fellowship Program
FY 2012 Funding $200,000
OJP Sponsor NIJ
Web Link www.nij.gov/funding/welcome.htm
Program Contact Marie Garcia, (202) 514–7128, Marie.Garcia@usdoj.gov; Gerald LaPorte, (202) 305-1106, Gerald.Laporte@usdoj.gov; Chris Tillery, (202) 305-9829, George.Tillery@usdoj.gov
Program Description
The NIJ Ph.D. Graduate Research Fellowship (GRF) program provides awards for research on crime, violence, and other criminal justice-related topics to accredited universities that offer research-based doctoral degrees. NIJ invests in doctoral education by supporting universities that sponsor students who demonstrate the potential to successfully complete doctoral degree programs in disciplines relevant to the mission of NIJ. Applicants sponsoring doctoral students in policy and health sciences or in an education field are eligible to apply only if the doctoral research dissertation is in a NIJ-supported discipline; i.e., social and behavioral sciences, operations technology, information and sensors research and development, and investigative and forensic sciences.

Program Name Building and Enhancing Criminal Justice Researcher-Practitioner Partnerships
FY 2012 Funding $1,000,000
OJP Sponsor NIJ
Web Link www.nij.gov/funding/welcome.htm
Program Contact Bethany Backes, (202) 305–4419, Bethany.Backes@usdoj.gov; Katharine Browning, (202) 616-4786, Katharine.Browning@usdoj.gov
Program Description

NIJ is interested in funding multiple research projects involving criminal justice researcher-practitioner partnerships, as well as capturing, in detail, relevant accounts of these collaborations. This solicitation specifically aims to support research and evaluation activities that include a researcher-practitioner partnership component. Within the context of the proposed research or evaluation project, these partnerships can be new or ongoing. Results from these projects should lead to better criminal justice policy, practice, and research, specifically as it relates to the participating practitioner partner.

Program Name W.E.B. Du Bois Fellowship for Research in Race, Gender, Culture, and Crime
FY 2012 Funding $200,000
OJP Sponsor NIJ
Web Link www.nij.gov/funding/welcome.htm
Program Contact Nadine Frederique, (202) 514-8777, Nadine.Frederique@usdoj.gov
Program Description
The W.E.B. Du Bois Fellowship for Research in Race, Gender, Culture, and Crime program seeks to advance knowledge regarding the convergence of crime, justice, and culture in various societal contexts. The Fellowship places particular emphasis on crime, violence, and the administration of justice in diverse cultural contexts within the United States.

Program Name Research and Evaluation in Justice Systems
FY 2012 Funding $1,850,000
OJP Sponsor NIJ
Web Link www.nij.gov/funding/welcome.htm
Program Contact Eric Martin, (202) 514-9588, Eric.D.Martin@usdoj.gov; Linda Truitt, (202)-353-9081, Linda.Truitt@usdoj.gov; Marie Garcia, (202) 514-7128, Marie.Garcia@usdoj.gov
Program Description
NIJ seeks proposals to examine topics relevant to state and/or local criminal and juvenile justice systems policy and practice. Specific focus areas under this solicitation include research on district attorneys' pretrial diversion programs; a pilot study on the impact of incarceration on families; and research on the impact of video visitation on offender outcomes.

Program Name Research and Evaluation on Trafficking in Persons
FY 2012 Funding $1,000,000
OJP Sponsor NIJ
Web Link www.nij.gov/funding/welcome.htm
Program Contact John Picarelli, (202) 307-3213, John.Picarelli@usdoj.gov
Program Description
NIJ seeks applications for research and evaluation studies on trafficking in persons (TIP) that can help federal, state, local, or tribal criminal justice agencies meet the challenge of TIP in their jurisdictions. NIJ is interested in studies that address: the under-reporting of trafficking cases at the federal, state and local levels of criminal justice; and the knowledge gaps related to trafficking in persons in the United States. NIJ also is interested in evaluation studies of counter-trafficking programs and tools.

Program Name Research on Domestic Radicalization
FY 2012 Funding $2,000,000
OJP Sponsor NIJ
Web Link www.nij.gov/funding/welcome.htm
Program Contact John Picarelli, (202) 307-3213, John.Picarelli@usdoj.gov
Program Description
NIJ seeks proposals for research on the phenomenon of domestic radicalization to violence. The focus of this solicitation is on all forms of domestic radicalization that lead to violent extremism. Specific focus areas under this solicitation include: empirical evaluation of theories of domestic radicalization; examination of radicalization processes for individuals; comparative analysis of violent extremists, organized criminals, gangs, hate groups and/or cults; and influence of community and other policing strategies on domestic radicalization to violence.

Program Name Desistance from Crime over the Life Course
FY 2012 Funding $1,000,000
OJP Sponsor NIJ
Web Link www.nij.gov/funding/welcome.htm
Program Contact Carrie Mulford, Social Science Analyst, (202) 307-2959,
Carrie.Mulford@usdoj.gov or Marie Garcia, (202) 514-7128, Marie.Garcia@usdoj.gov
Program Description
NIJ seeks proposals to conduct research that enhances knowledge of the process of desistance. NIJ encourages applicants to submit proposals for bold, innovative approaches to enhancing understanding of the processes underlying desistance from crime.

Program Name BJS Visiting Fellows
FY 2012 Funding $600,000
OJP Sponsor BJS
Web Link bjs.ojp.usdoj.gov
Program Contact Gerard Ramker, (202) 307-0765, Gerard.Ramker@usdoj.gov
Program Description
Under BJS sponsorship, selected fellows conduct studies on topics of their choosing that also support BJS goals and use BJS data. They interact with BJS staff and gain first-hand knowledge of some of the most recent developments in the field of criminal justice research. In addition to carrying out their research, fellows also have opportunities to contribute in other significant ways. For example, recent fellows have briefed the Attorney General on latest trends in youth violence, helped design a BJS survey on police use of force, explored new methods for visualizing BJS data, compared crime rates between the U.S. and England, and examined the methodological history of the NCVS. This program is open to senior level social science researchers whose work on crime-related subjects has been extensively published. Some fellows remain onsite at BJS for the entire duration of their project. Others make only occasional visits to accommodate their schedules. At the close of their visit, fellows prepare a research report summarizing results and policy implications of their project.

Program Name BJS Data Resource Center Program
FY 2012 Funding $1,500,000
OJP Sponsor BJS
Web Link bjs.ojp.usdoj.gov
Program Contact William Sabol, (202) 307-0765, William.Sabol@usdoj.gov
Program Description
BJS will seek to make a multi-year obligation to establish a BJS Data Resource Center at an institution of higher education or professional social science research organization that will provide analytical support to BJS and produce sponsored publications from available BJS data. The goal is to generate up to 10 products per year, as well as provide specific quantities of technical and methodological assistance, responses to requests, and empirical studies.

Section 2

Breaking the Cycles of Mental Illness, Substance Abuse, and Crime

Overview

Research shows that there are higher rates of substance abuse and mental illness among inmates and offenders than among the general population. The best data suggest that the relationship between drugs and crime is complex, mediated by the type of substance and its psychoactive effects, as well as personality factors, situational factors, and socio-cultural factors.

OJP, through a number of its bureaus, supports numerous programs and services to assist communities in planning, implementing, and enhancing criminal justice, substance abuse, and mental health partnerships, including specialized police responses, crisis response centers, problem solving courts, treatment within correctional facilities, and reentry services. Key components of these efforts include screening, assessment, testing, accountability, and follow-up.

In addition to investigating and deterring drug production, trafficking, and drug-related violence, OJP is interested in reducing criminal behavior through cost-efficient interventions designed to reduce alcohol and drug use among offenders. Program activities assist target population identification and support relapse and recidivism prevention. OJP also supports prescription drug monitoring programs that help detect and prevent the diversion and abuse of pharmaceutical controlled substances, particularly at the retail level, where no other automated information collection system exists. In addition, OJP surveys provide information about the prevalence of offenders with mental health disorders.

Discretionary Programs

Program Name Drug Court Discretionary Grant Program
FY 2012 Funding $24,675,453
OJP Sponsor BJA
Web Link www.bja.gov/funding.aspx
Program Contact Tim Jeffries, (202) 616-7385, Timothy.Jeffries@usdoj.gov
Program Description
This program will provide financial and technical assistance to states, state courts, local courts, and units of state, local, and tribal governments to implement and enhance drug treatment courts that effectively integrate substance abuse treatment, mandatory drug testing, sanctions and incentives, and transitional services in a judicially supervised court setting with jurisdiction over nonviolent, substance abusing offenders. Programs funded by Drug Court discretionary grants are required by law to target nonviolent offenders and must implement a drug court based on 10 key components. This program supports adult drug court implementation and enhancement and statewide drug court enhancement and coordination.

Program Name Harold Rogers Prescription Drug Monitoring Program (PDMP)
FY 2012 Funding $5,071,891
OJP Sponsor BJA
Web Link www.bja.gov/funding.aspx
Program Contact Danica Szarvas-Kidd, (202) 305-7418, Danica.Szarvas-Kidd@usdoj.gov
Program Description
This program enhances the capacity of regulatory and law enforcement agencies to collect and analyze controlled substance prescription data. The program supports states in establishing a prescription drug monitoring program. Resources are also available to states that want to expand their existing programs. Program objectives include the following:

- building a data collection and analysis system at the state level;
- enhancing existing programs' ability to analyze and use collected data;
- facilitating the exchange of collected prescription data among states; and
- assessing the efficiency and effectiveness of the programs funded under this initiative.

Program Name Justice and Mental Health Collaboration Program (JMHCP)
FY 2012 Funding $6,668,574
OJP Sponsor BJA
Web Link www.bja.gov/funding.aspx
Program Contact Danica Szarvas-Kidd, (202) 305-7418, Danica.Szarvas-Kidd@usdoj.gov
Program Description
This program increases public safety by facilitating collaboration among the criminal justice, juvenile justice, mental health treatment, and substance abuse systems to increase access to treatment for this unique group of offenders. The program

- increases public safety through early intervention for people with mental illness or a co-occurring disorder within the criminal or juvenile justice system;
- provides courts, including existing and new mental health courts, with appropriate mental health and substance abuse treatment options;
- maximizes the use of diversion from prosecution, alternative sentences through community supervision, and graduated sanctions, as appropriate, in cases involving nonviolent offenders with mental illness;
- promotes adequate training for criminal justice system personnel regarding mental illness and substance abuse disorders and the appropriate responses to people with such illnesses, including those with developmental and learning disabilities; and
- promotes adequate training for mental health and substance abuse treatment personnel regarding criminal offenders with mental illness or co-occurring substance abuse disorders and the appropriate response to such offenders in the criminal justice system.

*In FY 2011, BJA received 279 applications for funding under the Justice and Mental Health Collaboration Program (JMHCP), only 40 of which were awarded due to limited funding. In FY 2012, JMHCP faces further reductions to its appropriation. The peer review process in FY 2011 yielded a high number of qualified and competitive applications, many of which remain unfunded. The peer review process, while serving a valuable function in helping BJA staff make funding decisions, is also costly and is funded with JMHCP program funds. By relying on the peer review results of FY 2011 and forgoing a new competitive application process including peer review in FY 2012, BJA is able to maximize the number of awards made to the field. Therefore, BJA will not be issuing a FY 2012 JMHCP solicitation and instead will recommend FY 2012 JMHCP awards from the long list of unfunded, qualified, and highly competitive FY 2011 applications.

Training and Technical Assistance

Program Name Adult Drug Court Training Initiative
FY 2012 Funding $1,250,000
OJP Sponsor BJA
Web Link www.bja.gov/funding.aspx
Program Contact Tim Jeffries, (202) 616-7385, Timothy.Jeffries@usdoj.gov
Program Description
Through the Adult Drug Court Training Initiative, BJA provides culturally competent, interactive, drug court training services based on adult learning theory; develops and revises curricula for drug court practitioners; adjusts training delivery style based on the target audience size; develops and manages online training courses; and develops uniform protocols for evaluating and reporting on training services provided.

The BJA-approved drug court curricula accessible through this training initiative are Comprehensive Drug Court Judicial Training; Comprehensive Drug Court Coordinator Training; Comprehensive Drug Court Prosecutor Training; Comprehensive Drug Court Defense Attorney Training; Comprehensive Drug Court Treatment Provider Training; Comprehensive Drug Court Community Supervision Training; Comprehensive Drug Court Case Management Training; The Promise of Drug Court; Drug Court for Defense Counsel: A Paradigm Shift; Targeting and Eligibility; Psychopharmacology Treatment: What Works; Team Building; Confidentiality; Motivational Interviewing; Operational Tune-up Training; Incentives and Sanctions; Ensuring the Sustainability of Drug Court Programs; Supervising Methamphetamine Addicts in Drug Court; and Cultural Proficiency for Drug Court Practitioners.

Program Name Adult Drug Court Technical Assistance Program
FY 2012 Funding $1,200,000
OJP Sponsor BJA
Web Link www.bja.gov/funding.aspx
Program Contact Tim Jeffries, (202) 616-7385, Timothy.Jeffries@usdoj.gov
Program Description
The goal of this initiative is to assist operational adult drug treatment court programs in the development and implementation of improved program practices leading to greater program effectiveness and increased long-term participant success. The technical assistance provider serves both the BJA-funded adult implementation and enhancement drug court grantees, as well as other adult drug courts in the field.

Program Name Statewide Adult Drug Court Technical Assistance Program
FY 2012 Funding $250,000
OJP Sponsor BJA
Web Link www.bja.gov/funding.aspx
Program Contact Tim Jeffries, (202) 616-7385, Timothy.Jeffries@usdoj.gov
Program Description
This program provides direct aid and information to state agencies to enhance the leadership of the drug court effort in their states, improve coordination and collaboration among the drug court agencies, and increase the likelihood for the institutionalization of drug courts in mainstream court operations. The Statewide Adult Drug Court Technical Assistance provider serves those states that have received BJA Statewide Adult Drug Court Enhancement grants, as well as other states through the statewide drug/problem solving court coordinators.

Program Name Adult Drug Court Planning Initiative (DCPI)
FY 2012 Funding $1,600,000
OJP Sponsor BJA
Web Link www.bja.gov/funding.aspx
Program Contact Tim Jeffries, (202) 616-7385, Timothy.Jeffries@usdoj.gov
Program Description
DCPI consists of a standardized core curriculum based on adult learning theory and the 10 key components to support the implementation of adult drug courts. Each 5-day training event will host planning teams comprising a judge, prosecutor, defense attorney, treatment provider, coordinator, probation officer, law enforcement official, and evaluator.

DCPI also will engage mentor drug courts in the planning initiative. BJA and the training provider will jointly nominate and select exceptional drug courts to serve as mentors to new and operational courts. DCPI trainings may be hosted in or around the mentor courts so that newly forming teams can benefit from fully functioning, outcome oriented, drug court programs. BJA also has partnered with the Veterans Administration (VA) to develop a Veterans Court Planning Initiative to train existing drug court teams on how to capitalize on the substance abuse and mental health treatment, physical health services, housing subsidies, and skills training available through the VA. Additionally, tribal healing to wellness court teams will be trained on tribal drug court implementation.

Program Name National Drug Court Resource Center
FY 2012 Funding $400,000
OJP Sponsor BJA
Web Link www.bja.gov/funding.aspx
Program Contact Tim Jeffries, (202) 616-7385, Timothy.Jeffries@usdoj.gov
Program Description
The National Drug Court Resource Center collects, maintains, and disseminates information about drug court operations, best practices, trends, and history. Through the center, BJA compiles and continually updates information on national drug court activities and emerging issues, maintains an extensive reference collection of drug court materials, and serves the drug court field by providing comprehensive, timely responses to all relevant requests for drug court information.

Program Name Justice and Mental Health Collaboration Training and Technical Assistance Program
FY 2012 Funding $600,000
OJP Sponsor BJA
Web Link www.bja.gov/funding.aspx and http://consensusproject.org/issue_areas/justice-and-mental-health-collaboration-program
Program Contact Danica Szarvas-Kidd, (202) 305-7418, Danica.Szarvas-Kidd@usdoj.gov
Program Description
The training and technical assistance (TTA) partner will provide technical assistance to BJA's Justice and Mental Health Collaboration Program grantees that are planning, implementing, or expanding collaborative programs that improve responses to people with mental illnesses involved with the criminal justice system. TTA includes providing proactive, comprehensive, user-friendly TTA services; developing uniform protocols for the assessment and delivery of TTA, as well as tracking, evaluation, and follow-up; using TTA strategies that include developing tools and resources for grantees, such as distance learning, peer-to-peer consultations, onsite technical assistance, and ongoing technical assistance by phone and e-mail; and planning and hosting grantee meetings.

Program Name Justice and Mental Health Collaboration Program (JMHCP) State-Based Capacity Building Program (CBP)
FY 2012 Funding $525,000
OJP Sponsor BJA
Web Link www.bja.gov/funding.aspx
Program Contact Danica Szarvas-Kidd, (202) 305-7418, Danica.Szarvas-Kidd@usdoj.gov
Program Description
The primary goal of this program is to provide comprehensive resources and services to eligible but unfunded JMHCP grant applicants. The Council of State Governments Justice Center will serve as the primary source of information on justice and mental health collaboration programs and will implement strategies that include developing tools and resources such as distance learning; peer-to-peer consultations; and onsite, phone, and e-mail assistance to customers. In addition, the Justice Center will plan for a national conference that will focus on criminal justice and mental health collaborations.

Section 3

Preventing and Intervening in Juvenile Offending and Victimization

Overview

OJP provides targeted funding to enhance programs and collaborations that address juvenile offending and victimization through research and demonstration projects, training and technical assistance, and other information dissemination efforts.

Within OJP, the Office of Juvenile Justice and Delinquency Prevention (OJJDP) has primary responsibility for preventing and controlling juvenile delinquency, improving the juvenile justice system, and protecting children. Other OJP components also provide programming and research support for outreach to juveniles and their families.

OJP supports an array of activities that help states, tribal jurisdictions, and local governments meet the many juvenile justice challenges they face, including the following:

- holding juvenile offenders accountable for their unlawful actions;
- preparing juvenile offenders who are returning to their communities following release from secure correctional facilities;
- supporting evidence-based delinquency prevention programs and alternatives to detention;
- addressing juvenile gang activity and violence;
- addressing the disproportionate number of minority youth who come into contact with the juvenile justice system;
- combating juvenile alcohol and drug abuse; and
- helping children victimized by crime and abuse.

OJP programming strives to divert young people from the juvenile justice system, improve community safety, protect children from sexual predators, strengthen the juvenile justice system, and respond to childhood abuse, neglect, and victimization. The ultimate goal is to support young people in their efforts to become productive, contributing members of their communities.

Discretionary Programs

Program Name Community-Based Violence Prevention Program
FY 2012 Funding $6,000,000
OJP Sponsor OJJDP
Web Link www.ojjdp.gov
Program Contact Dennis Mondoro, (202) 514-3913, Dennis.Mondoro@ usdoj.gov; Jeffrey Gersh, (202) 514-5535, Jeffrey.Gersh@usdoj.gov
Program Description
OJJDP will fund new sites to replicate intervention programs, such as the Boston Gun Project, the Richmond Comprehensive Homicide Initiative, and the Chicago CeaseFire model, to reduce violence in targeted communities. Applicants must focus their proposed programs on the high-risk activities and behaviors of a small number of carefully selected members of the community who are likely to be involved in gun violence in the immediate future. The intervention with this target population should include improved coordination of existing resources and activities that support multiple, complementary anti-violence strategies.

Program Name Defending Childhood Task Force Recommendation Technical Assistance
FY 2012 Funding $2,400,000
OJP Sponsor OJJDP
Web Link www.justice.gov/defendingchildhood/task-force.html
Program Contact Will Bronson, (202) 305-2427, Willie.Bronson@usdoj.gov
Program Description
OJJDP will fund an organization or a consortium of organizations to provide resources and technical assistance to state and local governments to implement recommendations that the Attorney General's Task Force on Children Exposed to Violence will propose. The task force is presently conducting four public hearings around the country to gather testimony from experts, advocates, and impacted families and communities on the extent, nature, and consequences of children's exposure to violence, abuse, and crime in the United States. The task force will issue a final report to the Attorney General late in 2012 that presents its findings and comprehensive policy recommendations.

Program Name Enforcing Underage Drinking Laws (EUDL) Program
FY 2012 Funding $2,700,000
OJP Sponsor OJJDP
Web Link
www.ojjdp.gov/programs/ProgSummary.asp?pi=17&ti=&si=&kw=&PreviousPage=ProgResults
Program Contact Sharie Cantelon, (202) 616-3658, Sharie.Cantelon@usdoj.gov
Program Description
OJJDP will support discretionary grants and technical assistance under the EUDL program. The EUDL discretionary grant component supports several initiatives to help communities develop a comprehensive approach to address underage drinking. EUDL training and technical assistance supports communities and states in their efforts to enforce underage drinking laws.

Program Name Second Chance Act Adult and Juvenile Offender Reentry Demonstration Projects
FY 2012 Funding $1,200,000
OJP Sponsor OJJDP
Web Link www.bja.gov/funding.aspx
Program Contact Thomas Murphy, (202) 353-8734, Thomas.Murphy@usdoj.gov
Program Description
OJJDP, in collaboration with BJA, will support additional demonstration projects under the Second Chance Act Youth Offender Reentry Initiative, a comprehensive response to the increasing number of people who are released from prison, jail, and juvenile facilities each year and are returning to their communities. The goal of this initiative is to reduce the rate of recidivism for offenders released from a juvenile residential facility and increase public safety. Demonstration projects provide necessary services to youth while in confinement and following their release into the community. The initiative will focus on addressing the unique needs of girls reentering their communities.

Program Name Family Drug Court Programs
FY 2012 Funding $2,300,000
OJP Sponsor OJJDP
Web Link www.ojjdp.gov/
Program Contact Gwendolyn Williams, (202) 616-1611, Gwendolyn.Williams@usdoj.gov
Program Description
OJJDP will implement and enhance family drug courts that serve substance-abusing adults, who are involved in the family dependency court system as a result of child abuse and neglect issues. Grantees must provide services to the children of the parents in the program, as well as to the parents.

Program Name Internet Crimes Against Children Commercial Child Sexual Exploitation
FY 2012 Funding $20,000,000
OJP Sponsor OJJDP
Web Link www.ojjdp.gov

Program Contact Child Protection Division, (202) 616-3637
Program Description
OJJDP will support select law enforcement agencies in their development of strategies to protect children from commercial sexual exploitation. Grantees will improve training and coordination activities, develop policies and procedures to identify child victims of commercial sexual exploitation, investigate and prosecute cases against adults who sexually exploit children for commercial purposes, and provide essential services to victims, including cases where technology is used to facilitate the exploitation of the victim.

Program Name Multi-State Mentoring Programs
FY 2012 Funding $10,000,000
OJP Sponsor OJJDP
Web Link www.ojjdp.gov
Program Contact Kerri Strug, (202) 305-0702, Kerri.Strug@usdoj.gov
Program Description
OJJDP will support organizations with mentoring programs in at least five states to enhance or expand mentoring services to high-risk populations that are underserved due to location; shortage of mentors; special physical or mental challenges of the targeted population; youth with a parent in the military, including a deployed parent; or other analogous situations that the community in need of mentoring services identifies.

Program Name National Mentoring Programs
FY 2012 Funding $50,000,000
OJP Sponsor OJJDP
Web Link www.ojjdp.gov
Program Contact Jennifer Yeh, (202) 616-9135, Jennifer.Yeh2@usdoj.gov
Program Description
OJJDP will support national organizations to enhance or expand mentoring services to high-risk populations that are underserved due to location; shortage of mentors; special physical or mental challenges of the targeted population; youth with a parent in the military, including a deployed parent; or other analogous situations that the community in need of mentoring services identifies.

Program Name Multi-Site Mentoring Enhancement Demonstration Project
FY 2012 Funding $4,000,000
OJP Sponsor OJJDP
Web Link www.ojjdp.gov
Program Contact Jennifer Tyson, (202) 305-1598, Jennifer.Tyson@usdoj.gov; Michael Shader, (202) 616-2605, Michael.Shader@usdoj.gov
Program Description
OJJDP will support a Mentoring Enhancement Demonstration Project consisting of a multi-site mentoring enhancement implementation and an evaluation to measure the effectiveness of the mentoring enhancement. Grantees would provide enhanced mentoring services for approximately 100 youth at each of three to four sites. The evaluation component will then assess whether implementing this evidence-based enhancement improved the effectiveness of the services and the outcomes for youth.

Program Name National Intertribal Youth Summit
FY 2012 Funding $500,000
OJP Sponsor OJJDP
Web Link www.ojjdp.gov
Program Contact James Antal, (202) 514-1289, James.Antal@usdoj.gov
Program Description
OJJDP will support the 2012 National Intertribal Youth Summit that will develop and implement a culturally sensitive youth leadership agenda for at-risk American Indian and Alaska Native youth that focuses on critical issues in tribal communities. The conference will target leadership

development and examine critical tribal youth issues, such as teen dating violence, substance abuse, suicide, delinquency, and gang involvement.

Training and Technical Assistance

Program Name National Forum on Youth Violence Prevention Training and Technical Assistance
FY 2012 Funding $900,000
OJP Sponsor OJJDP
Web Link www.ojjdp.gov
Program Contact James Antal, (202) 514-1289, James.Antal@usdoj.gov
Program Description
OJJDP will fund an organization or a consortium of organizations to provide training and technical assistance to the six cities (Boston, Chicago, Detroit, Memphis, Salinas, and San Jose) participating in the National Forum on Youth Violence Prevention. Created at the direction of the President, the forum is a working team of seven federal agencies (Justice; Education; Health and Human Services, Centers for Disease Control; Labor; Housing and Urban Development; and the Office of National Drug Control Policy). Participating localities share their challenges and promising strategies in fighting youth violence and gang activity and explore how federal agencies can better support local efforts to address these problems. Local stakeholders include public health officials and representatives from the mayor/city manager's office, schools, law enforcement, and the local office of the U.S. Attorney.

Research and Statistical Programs

Program Name Mentoring Research Best Practices Program
FY 2012 Funding $2,700,000
OJP Sponsor OJJDP
Web Link www.ojjdp.gov
Program Contact Jennifer Tyson, (202) 305-1598, Jennifer.Tyson@usdoj.gov; Michael Shader, (202) 616-2605, Michael.Shader@usdoj.gov
Program Description
OJJDP will fund a program of research that seeks to enhance the understanding of mentoring as a prevention strategy for youth at risk of involvement or already involved in the juvenile justice system. While mentoring appears to be a promising intervention for youth, more evaluation work is needed to further highlight the components of a mentoring program that are most effective and determine the effectiveness of mentoring as a delinquency prevention and intervention technique.

Program Name Tribal Youth Field-Initiated Research and Evaluation Program
FY 2012 Funding $1,000,000
OJP Sponsor OJJDP
Web Link www.ojjdp.gov
Program Contact Barbara Kelley, (202) 616-9517, Barbara.Kelley@usdoj.gov
Program Description
OJJDP will fund a field-initiated study to further what is understood regarding the experiences, strengths, and needs of tribal youth, their families, and communities and what works to reduce their risks for delinquency and victimization. Accordingly, OJJDP will seek applications addressing a broad range of research topics, such as the identification of risk factors for delinquent behavior and substance abuse, pathways to delinquency and desistance, and victimization experiences among tribal youth.

Program Name Field-Initiated Research and Evaluation Program
FY 2012 Funding $1,500,000
OJP Sponsor OJJDP
Web Link www.ojjdp.gov
Program Contact Brecht Donoghue, (202) 305-1270, Brecht.Donoghue@usdoj.gov
Program Description

OJJDP will support multiple grant awards for research and evaluations of school-based practices, environment, and achievement that relate to reducing student victimization and the risk of delinquency. OJJDP will support research that investigates how to improve the level and quality of a juvenile's participation in school. OJJDP is also interested in ways to improve school safety and climate. Additionally, OJJDP is looking for research on how to stem the "school-to-prison pipeline;" to increase accessibility of quality education for all youth, including juvenile offenders; and to advance use of positive discipline and learning policies and practices nationwide.

Program Name National Juvenile Court Data Archive
FY 2012 Funding $600,000
OJP Sponsor OJJDP
Web Link www.ojjdp.gov/ojstatbb/default.asp
Program Contact Brecht Donoghue, (202) 305-1270, Brecht.Donoghue@usdoj.gov
Program Description
OJJDP will support the National Juvenile Court Data Archive, which provides the most detailed information available on the activities of the nation's juvenile courts to juvenile justice professionals, policymakers, researchers, and the public. The Archive pursues three general goals: data collection and processing, data use and dissemination, and data improvement.

Program Name Enforcing Underage Drinking Laws Field-Initiated Research and Evaluation Program
FY 2012 Funding $600,000
OJP Sponsor OJJDP
Web Link www.ojjdp.gov
Program Contact Brecht Donoghue, (202) 305-1270, Brecht.Donoghue@usdoj.gov
Program Description
OJJDP will support field-initiated studies to understand the factors that influence the prevention of underage drinking, the enforcement of underage drinking laws, and individuals' and communities' attitudes and behaviors about underage drinking. Applicants must clearly indicate a central research question and propose a comprehensive and logical research methodology. Additionally, applicants should clearly articulate how the proposed study will fill a gap in the research on underage drinking prevention and/or enforcement and how the anticipated findings will inform state and local efforts to enforce underage drinking laws.

Program Name Community-Based Violence Prevention Field-Initiated Research and Evaluation Program
FY 2012 Funding $750,000
OJP Sponsor OJJDP
Web Link www.ojjdp.gov
Program Contact Brecht Donoghue, (202) 305-1270, Brecht.Donoghue@usdoj.gov
Program Description
OJJDP will support field-initiated studies to inform what is understood about how communities can prevent and reduce violence involving youth. OJJDP is looking to improve the available research about the factors that may influence youth violence and youth violence prevention efforts, assess the effectiveness and cost efficiency of existing community-based violence prevention programs, and identify and evaluate new or emerging community-based violence prevention models.

Program Name Research and Evaluation on Children Exposed to Violence
FY 2012 Funding $1,000,000
OJP Sponsor NIJ
Web Link www.nij.gov/nij/funding/forthcoming.htm
Program Contact Dara Blachman-Demner, (202) 514-9528, Dara.Blachman-Demner@usdoj.gov
Program Description
NIJ seeks proposals for research related to childhood exposure to violence. In particular, NIJ

seeks proposals that address resilience, poly-victimization, electronic aggression, or justice system responses to children identified as exposed to violence.

Program Name Evaluation of the Office of Juvenile Justice and Delinquency Prevention FY 2010 Second Chance Act Juvenile Offender Reentry Demonstration Projects
FY 2012 Funding $2,500,000
OJP Sponsor NIJ
Web Link www.nij.gov/nij/funding/forthcoming.htm
Program Contact Donna Davis, (202) 514-9331, Donna.Davis@usdoj.gov.
Program Description
NIJ seeks applications for a comprehensive evaluation of a subset of juvenile reentry demonstration projects funded under the Second Chance Chance Act of 2007. This solicitation seeks to award a grant in order to measure the processes, outcomes, costs, and impacts of the juvenile offender reentry programs that received funding under the Second Chance Act in FY2009 and FY2010 and to assess the effectiveness of the Second Chance Act in reducing recidivism among juvenile offenders.

Section 4

Managing Offenders to Reduce Recidivism and Promote Successful Reentry

Overview

In 2008, more than 7.3 million people were on probation, in jail or prison, or on parole at yearend — 3.2 percent of all U.S. adult residents or one in every 31 adults. About 70 percent of the persons under correctional supervision at yearend 2008 were supervised in the community, either on probation or parole, while 30 percent were incarcerated in the nation's prisons or jails.

These individuals face multiple barriers to leading crime-free lives including mental illness, substance abuse, health problems, poor employment histories, family issues, lack of job skills, and lack of housing, as well as other significant personal problems. Research shows that about two-thirds of offenders are rearrested within three years of release, and half return to prison during that same period.

OJP, through a number of its bureaus, is working to reduce recidivism and its attendant fiscal and social costs and increase the safety of our communities. One of the largest efforts is the administration of the Second Chance Act of 2007.

Through the provisions of this statute, OJP is able to increase its support of reentry demonstration projects that use validated assessment tools to determine the risks and needs of offenders. BJA is overseeing projects designed to provide offenders in prisons or jails with necessary services. These include educational, literacy, vocational, and job placement services that facilitate reentry into the community; substance abuse treatment and services during incarceration that continue in community-based settings upon an offender's release; and coordinated supervision and comprehensive services for offenders upon release from prison or jail, including housing and mental and physical health care to include veteran specific services.

OJP addresses the challenges that returning sex offenders bring to their communities through the Adam Walsh Act Implementation Grant Program. This program assists states, the District of Columbia, territories, and tribal jurisdictions with developing and/or enhancing programs designed to implement the requirements of the Sex Offender Registration and Notification Act (SORNA) of the Adam Walsh Child Protection and Safety Act of 2006, and to promote innovation and best practices in the field of sex offender management.

Discretionary Programs

Program Name Second Chance Act Adult and Juvenile Offender Reentry Demonstration Projects (Section 101)
FY 2012 Funding $6,400,000
OJP Sponsor BJA
Web Link www.bja.gov/funding.aspx
Program Contact Gary Dennis, (202) 305-9059, Gary.Dennis@usdoj.gov; Thurston Bryant, (202) 514-8082, Thurston.Bryant@usdoj.gov
Program Description
The Second Chance Act authorizes grants to state and local governments and federally recognized Indian tribes for demonstration projects to promote the safe and successful reintegration of incarcerated individuals into the community. Allowable funding uses include employment services, substance abuse treatment, housing, family programming, mentoring, victim services, methods to improve release and revocation decisions using risk assessment tools, and other services.

Program Name Second Chance Mentoring Program (Section 211)
FY 2012 Funding $5,600,000*
OJP Sponsor BJA
Web Link www.bja.gov/funding.aspx
Program Contact Gary Dennis, (202) 305-9059, Gary.Dennis@usdoj.gov; Thurston Bryant, (202) 514-8082, Thurston.Bryant@usdoj.gov
Program Description
The Second Chance Act authorizes mentoring grants for nonprofit organizations and federally recognized Indian tribes. Project initiatives include mentoring adult offenders and offering transitional or other services to promote the safe and successful reintegration of formerly incarcerated individuals back into the community.

*The peer review process in FY 2011 yielded a high number of qualified and competitive applications, many of which remain unfunded. The peer review process, while serving a valuable function in assisting BJA staff make funding decisions, is also costly and is funded with Second Chance Act program funds. By relying on the peer review results of FY 2011 and forgoing a new competitive application process including peer review in FY 2012, BJA is able to maximize the number of awards made to the field. Therefore, BJA will not be issuing a FY 2012 Second Chance Act Mentoring solicitation and instead will recommend FY 2012 Second Chance Act mentoring awards from the list of unfunded, qualified, and highly competitive FY 2011 applications.

Program Name Second Chance Act Family-Based Prisoner Substance Abuse Treatment Program (Section 113)
FY 2012 Funding $2,400,000
OJP Sponsor BJA
Web Link www.bja.gov/funding.aspx
Program Contact Gary Dennis, (202) 305-9059, Gary.Dennis@usdoj.gov; Thurston Bryant, (202) 514-8082, Thurston.Bryant@usdoj.gov
Program Description
Section 113 of the Second Chance Act authorizes grants to states, units of local government, and Indian tribes to improve the provision of substance abuse treatment within prisons and jails and after reentry for inmates who have minor children. It also includes outreach to families and provision of treatment and other services to children and other family members of participant inmates. BJA is seeking applications from eligible applicants to plan, implement, or expand such treatment programs.

Program Name Second Chance Act Technology Careers Training Demonstration Projects for Incarcerated Adults and Juveniles (Section 115)
FY 2012 Funding $3,000,000
OJP Sponsor BJA
Web Link www.bja.gov/funding.aspx
Program Contact Gary Dennis, (202) 305-9059, Gary.Dennis@usdoj.gov; Thurston Bryant, (202) 514-8082, Thurston.Bryant@usdoj.gov
Program Description
Section 115 of the Second Chance Act authorizes the Attorney General to make federal awards to states, units of local government, territories, and federally recognized Indian tribes to provide technology career training to incarcerated adults and juveniles.

Program Name Second Chance Act Co-Occurring Substance Abuse and Mental Health Disorders (Section 201)
FY 2012 Funding $6,000,000
OJP Sponsor BJA
Web Link www.bja.gov/funding.aspx
Program Contact Gary Dennis, (202) 305-9059, Gary.Dennis@usdoj.gov; Thurston Bryant,

(202) 514-8082, Thurston.Bryant@usdoj.gov

Program Description

Section 201 of the Second Chance Act authorizes grants to states, units of local government, territories, and Indian tribes to improve the provision of drug treatment to offenders in prisons, jails, and juvenile facilities during the period of incarceration and through the completion of parole or other court supervision after release into the community. BJA is seeking applications from eligible applicants to implement or expand offender treatment programs for re-entering offenders with co-occurring substance abuse and mental health disorders.

Program Name SMART Promoting Evidence Integration in Sex Offender Management: Circles of Support and Accountability for Project Sites

FY 2012 Funding $600,000

OJP Sponsor SMART Office

Web Link www.smart.gov

Program Contact Scott Matson, (202) 305-4560, Scott.Matson@usdoj.gov; Jackie O'Reilly, (202) 514-5024, Jacqueline.O'Reilly@usdoj.gov

Program Description

The goal of Circles of Support and Accountability (COSA) is to fund up to three project sites to substantially reduce the risk of future sexual victimization of community members by assisting and supporting released men in their task of integrating with the community and leading responsible, productive, and accountable lives. The COSA initiative serves as a means to fill a gap in supervision for those high-risk sex offenders who "max-out" their incarcerative sentences and are released into the community without a formal process of aftercare. This project will provide funding to support the development or enhancement of COSA programs in jurisdictions.

Program Name SMART Promoting Evidence Integration in Sex Offender Management: Implementing Sites of the Sex Offender Treatment Intervention and Progress Scale Project

FY 2012 Funding $675,000

OJP Sponsor SMART Office

Web Link www.smart.gov

Program Contact Jackie O'Reilly, (202) 514-5024, Jacqueline.O'Reilly@usdoj.gov

Program Description

The goal of the Sex Offender Treatment Intervention and Progress Scale Project for implementing sites is to fund up to three sites to enhance sex offender management strategies in jurisdictions through supporting the development of a sex offender risk assessment model that combines the use of static and dynamic risk assessment tools in the management of sex offenders. Implementing sites will incorporate the use of specific static and dynamic sex offender risk assessment tools in their sex offender assessment and supervision practices. Data on the combined use of these tools will be collected and evaluated to determine whether the use of both static and dynamic risk assessment tools increases the predictive accuracy of the tools.

Program Name Second Chance Act Demonstration Field Experiment: Fostering Desistance through Effective Supervision

FY 2012 Funding $4,000,000

OJP Sponsor BJA

Web Link www.bja.gov/funding.aspx

Program Contact Ed Banks, (202) 307-3081, Edward.Banks@usdoj.gov

Program Description

This Demonstration Field Experiment (DFE) will focus on techniques to improve an offender's motivation to change, and strategies to alter criminal thinking using a desistance approach. The multi-site DFE also will provide a rigorous test of a specific reentry model intended to improve offender outcomes post-release. Some of the outcomes of interest include, but are not limited to, re-offending and re-incarceration (recidivism).

The goals of the program are to (1) improve the offender's motivation to change; (2) address cognitive and behavioral functioning regarding crime-prone thoughts and behaviors; and (3) address core criminogenic needs that affect an offender's performance while on parole. The model also works on building the infrastructure of the reentry process and community-based services to deliver collaborative and seamless services.

Program Name Smart Probation: Reducing Prison Populations, Saving Money, and Creating Safer Communities
FY 2012 Funding $2,875,366
OJP Sponsor BJA
Web Link www.bja.gov
Program Contact Gary Dennis, (202) 305-9059, Gary.Dennis@usdoj.gov
Program Description
The grants and technical assistance provided to jurisdictions (state, local, and tribal) by this initiative will be focused on six priority areas:

- building capacity in states to help local probation improve supervision strategies and reduce recidivism;
- providing demonstration grants to local probation agencies and court systems that will advance new strategies in probation to increase public safety and generate savings;
- developing and promoting knowledge and expertise that will make probation supervision more effective;
- promoting the integration of probation supervision strategies and services;
- increasing collaboration and strategic partnerships between probation and local law enforcement; and
- evaluating selected sites (jurisdictions) that receive targeted funding under the initiative to assess how well the interventions developed and policy changes implemented have helped the jurisdictions.

Program Name PREA Demonstration Projects to Establish "Zero Tolerance" Cultures for Sexual Assault Program (Prison Rape Prevention and Prosecution Program)
FY 2012 Funding $6,210,519
OJP Sponsor BJA
Web Link www.bja.gov/funding.aspx
Program Contact Gary Dennis, (202) 305-9059, Gary.Dennis@usdoj.gov; Thurston Bryant, (202) 514-8082, Thurston.Bryant@usdoj.gov
Program Description
As a result of the 2003 Prison Rape Elimination Act (PREA), BJA established the Protecting Inmates and Safeguarding Communities Program in FY 2004. Funding was made available to states to support efforts to prevent and eliminate prisoner rape between inmates in state and local prisons, jails, and police lockup facilities and to safeguard the communities to which inmates return. The two main goals of the Protecting Inmates and Safeguarding Communities Program are to assist states and local jurisdictions in ensuring that budget cuts not compromise efforts to protect inmates, and to safeguard communities upon the inmate's reentry. Applicants may apply for funding under the Protecting Inmates portion, the Safeguarding Communities portion, or both.

Program Name State Criminal Alien Assistance Program (SCAAP)
FY 2012 Funding $215,721,966
OJP Sponsor BJA
Web Link www.bja.gov/funding.aspx
Program Contact Joe Husted, (202) 353-4411, Joseph.Husted@usdoj.gov
Program Description
BJA administers SCAAP, in conjunction with the Bureau of Citizenship and Immigration Services, Department of Homeland Security (DHS). SCAAP, limited to eligible jurisdictions in all states, cities and counties, provides federal payments to states and localities that incurred correctional officer salary costs for incarcerating undocumented criminal aliens with at least one felony or two misdemeanor convictions for violations of state or local law, and incarcerated for at least 4 consecutive days during the reporting period.

Program Name Evaluation of the FY 2011 Bureau of Justice Assistance Second Chance Act Adult Reentry Program for Planning and Demonstration Projects
FY 2012 Funding $3,000,000
OJP Sponsor NIJ
Web Link www.nij.gov/funding/welcome.htm
Program Contact Marie Garcia, (202) 514-7128, Marie.Garcia@usdoj.gov
Program Description
NIJ is interested in funding proposals for a comprehensive evaluation of adult demonstration projects funded under the Second Chance Act of 2007. This solicitation seeks to award a grant in order to measure the processes, outcomes, costs, and impacts of the adult offender reentry programs that received funding under the Second Chance Act in FY 2011 and to assess the effectiveness of the Second Chance Act in reducing recidivism among released prisoners.

Training and Technical Assistance

Program Name SMART Promoting Evidence Integration in Sex Offender Management: Circles of Support and Accountability Training and Technical Assistance Program
FY 2012 Funding $500,000
OJP Sponsor SMART Office
Web Link www.smart.gov
Program Contact Scott Matson, (202) 305-4560, Scott.Matson@usdoj.gov; Jackie O'Reilly, (202) 514-5024, Jacqueline.O'Reilly@ojp.usdoj.gov
Program Description
The goal of Circles of Support and Accountability (COSA) is to substantially reduce the risk of future sexual victimization of community members by assisting and supporting released men in their task of integrating with the community and leading responsible, productive, and accountable lives. The COSA initiative serves as a means to fill a gap in supervision for those high-risk sex offenders who "max-out" their incarcerative sentences and are released into the community without a formal process of aftercare. Funds also will be used to provide training and technical assistance to sites as they work to locate and train volunteers or expand their existing COSA programs.

Program Name SMART Promoting Evidence Integration in Sex Offender Management: Sex Offender Treatment Intervention and Progress Scale Training and Technical Assistance Project
FY 2012 Funding $225,000
OJP Sponsor SMART Office
Web Link www.smart.gov
Program Contact Jackie O'Reilly, (202) 514-5024, Jacqueline.O'Reilly@ojp.usdoj.gov
Program Description
The goal of this program is to provide training and technical assistance to the competitively selected Sex Offender Treatment Intervention and Progress Scale implementing sites on a sex offender risk assessment model that combines the use of specific static and dynamic risk assessment tools. The grantee will provide specific training and technical assistance on administering, scoring, and interpreting these tools.

Program Name SMART FY 2012 Professional Development Fellowship Program
FY 2012 Funding $450,000 (up to $150,000 per fellow)
OJP Sponsor SMART Office
Web Link www.smart.gov
Program Contact Dawn Doran, (202) 353-3040, Dawn.Doran@usdoj.gov; Faith Baker, (202) 305-2586, Faith.Baker@usdoj.gov
Program Description
The SMART Office proposes to fund for the first time three fellowship positions to enhance the capacity of the SMART Office by providing technical assistance and support to state, local and tribal jurisdictions on their responses to sexual violence and exploitation in the context of sex offender management. The fellowships will focus on 1) victims' issues, 2) prevention and

education, and 3) practices and research in Indian Country in the field of sex offender management. The goal of these fellowships will be to work on multi-disciplinary issues with the relevant program offices within the Office of Justice Programs (Office of Victims of Crime, the Office of Juvenile Justice and Delinquency Prevention, the Bureau of Justice Assistance, the National institute of Justice, and the Bureau of Justice Statistics), as well as the Office on Violence Against Women, to explore and build a foundation within the field of sex offender management for the integration of effective victim-centered approaches, prevention and education programming, and sexual violence prevention and sex offender management programming in Indian Country.

Research and Statistical Programs

Program Name Determining the Relationship between Stress and Unexplained In-Custody Deaths
FY 2012 Funding $400,000
OJP Sponsor NIJ
Web Link www.nij.gov/funding/welcome.htm
Program Contact Brian Montgomery, (202) 353-9726, Brian.Montgomery@usdoj.gov
Program Description
NIJ will fund research that examines whether the physiologic and metabolic effects of the stress of being subdued or restrained, by any means, may explain otherwise unexplained in-custody deaths. Specifically, NIJ seeks proposals for research to: (1) clarify the fatal mechanisms that might be associated with stress resulting from subdual and restraint, by any means and not limited to CEDs; and, if such mechanisms can be demonstrated, (2) identify post-mortem markers that can inform death investigations.

Program Name Evaluation of the Implementation of the Sex Offender Treatment Intervention and Progress Scale
Grantee Competitive
FY 2012 Funding $1,000,000
OJP Sponsor NIJ
Web Link www.nij.gov/nij/funding/forthcoming.htm
Program Contact Marie Garcia, (202) 514-7128, Marie.Garcia@usdoj.gov
Program Description
NIJ seeks applications for a study to replicate the use of Vermont's Dynamic Risk Assessment Tool. Interested applicants will be required to evaluate the risk assessment tool in one jurisdiction (to be determined).

Section 5

Effective Interventions to Address Violence, Victimization, and Victims' Rights

Overview

OVC is charged by Congress with the administration of the Crime Victims Fund, the bedrock of federal funding for victim services across the nation. OVC manages two major funding streams that channel formula grants to states and territories to provide compensation and assistance to victims. OVC also supports national scope demonstration projects, training and technical assistance, and other capacity building programs to strengthen the knowledge and skills of service providers, advocates, and others who are committed to ensuring justice for all victims of crime.

OVC is challenged by an increased demand for services and rapidly changing social realities—from new technologies to shifting demographic trends. A critical aspect of OJP's capacity building strategy is a reliance on research to guide planning and set priorities, emphasizing evidence-based, culturally competent, victim-centered programs and services. In 2012, OVC will continue to build on the strategically planned programs, projects, and activities, initially funded in 2011, that have proven to be efficiently managed and effective in targeting specific needs of victims. These programs, funded by discretionary grants, will help strengthen established support for victims, including those historically underserved because of race, age, socio-economic status, disability, or sexual orientation—many of whom experience high rates of victimization. This continued focus will help to ensure that more victims of crime receive the skilled, compassionate care they need and deserve.

OVC's strategy for building the field's capacity to serve victims incorporates an increased reliance on dynamic, multidisciplinary partnerships. In 2012, OVC will continue its support of action partnerships, with a special emphasis on poly-victimization. In collaboration with federal and other partners, OVC will continue to address identity theft and financial fraud through public awareness and support to practitioners and to support those in the field who combat human trafficking. The enduring challenge of improving culturally sensitive services to victims in Indian Country remains a high priority. Also, as access to legal services is essential to ensuring justice for victims, OVC is supporting the development of wraparound legal assistance demonstration programs. Additional expertise in many of these areas is provided by OVC's visiting fellows program, which brings victim service specialists from across the country to Washington, DC to support OVC's mission.

Discretionary Programs

Program Name Action Partnerships for Membership, Professional, and Community Service Organizations Responding to Poly-Victimization Issues
FY 2012 Funding $1,500,000
OJP Sponsor OVC
Web Link www.ovc.gov
Program Contacts Jasmine D'Addario-Fobian, (202) 305-3332, jasmine.d'addario-fobian@usdoj.gov; Sharron Chapman, (202) 305-2358, Sharron.Chapman@usdoj.gov
Program Description
This program develops and/or improves the capacity of members of national membership, professional, and community service organizations to advance victims' rights and improve victims' services, with a focus on poly-victimization. The purpose of this cooperative agreement is to create partnerships among OVC, the victim services field, and national scope membership, professional, and community service organizations to advance victims' rights and services

through training, public awareness, and educational efforts. OVC anticipates funding up to six cooperative agreements of up to $250,000 each.

Program Name Wraparound Victim Legal Assistance Network Demonstration Project
FY 2012 Funding $2,400,000
OJP Sponsor OVC
Web Link www.ovc.gov
Program Contact Meg Morrow (202) 307-5983, Meg.Morrow@usdoj.gov
Program Description
This demonstration project will fund up to six sites to develop comprehensive, wraparound, pro bono legal assistance networks to meet the wide range of legal needs of crime victims. The networks funded under this demonstration project will develop collaborative models, in jurisdictions of various sizes, for fully meeting a victim's legal needs -- models that may be replicated in other jurisdictions of similar sizes around the country. Legal services will include civil legal assistance (including but not limited to family, custody and dependency, tribal, employment, and administrative issues related to the victimization); enforcement of victims' rights in criminal proceedings; assistance for victims of financial fraud; and immigration assistance for human trafficking victims and battered immigrant women.

Program Name Identifying Culturally Responsive Victim-Centered Restorative Justice (VCRJ) Strategies
FY 2012 Funding $250,000
OJP Sponsor OVC
Web Link www.ovc.gov
Program Contact Mary Atlas-Terry, (202) 353-8473, mary.atlas-terry@usdoj.gov; Kathleen Gless, (202) 307-6049, Kathleen.Gless@usdoj.gov
Program Description
This program will support a national assessment of current victim-centered restorative justice practices, such as traditional peacemaking or peacekeeping strategies, with an emphasis on practices implemented in tribal and urban inner city areas. The analysis and assessment of current programs and the subsequent written report will help OVC develop a demonstration site designed to implement and evaluate promising victim-centered models. The development of VCRJ models may help communities to support victims in their recovery by providing more procedural and distributive fairness to victims without interfering with offenders' rights or public safety.

Program Name Victim Assistance Professional Development Fellowship Program – Financial Fraud and Abuse Fellowship
FY 2012 Funding $135,000
OJP Sponsor OVC
Web Link www.ovc.gov
Program Contact Meg Morrow, (202) 307-5983, Meg.Morrow@usdoj.gov
Program Description
This competitive program will award one fellowship to enhance OVC's efforts to facilitate the understanding, development, or enhancement of innovative programs, models, practices, and protocols that serve crime victims. The fellow will focus on financial fraud and abuse, with a major focus on elder financial exploitation. Additionally, the fellowship will address financial abuse including identity theft, which is closely connected to other types of victimization, such as domestic violence and child abuse.

Program Name Services for Victims of Human Trafficking
FY 2012 Funding $TBD
OJP Sponsor OVC
Web Link www.ovc.gov
Program Contact Brad Mitchell, (202) 514-9069, Bradley.Mitchell@usdoj.gov
Program Description

This program provides funding to victim service organizations with a demonstrated history of providing trauma-informed, culturally competent services to male and female victims of sex trafficking and labor trafficking. Funding under this program will support either a comprehensive array of services for trafficking victims in specific geographic areas or specialized mental health or legal services over larger geographic areas. Funding also will support efforts to increase the capacity of communities to respond to victims through the development of interagency partnerships and public outreach and awareness campaigns.

Program Name Services for Victims of Human Trafficking Fellowship Program
FY 2012 Funding $135,000
OJP Sponsor OVC
Web Link www.ovc.gov
Program Contact Brad Mitchell, (202) 514-9069, Bradley.Mitchell@usdoj.gov
Program Description
This competitive program will award one fellowship to assist OVC in its ongoing efforts to advance services for victims of human trafficking within the United States. The fellow will support the administration of OVC's Services for Victims of Human Trafficking Program along with all associated training, technical assistance, and outreach efforts dedicated toward victim service professionals, law enforcement, and allied professionals. The fellow will undertake special projects that support OVC, OJP, and DOJ leadership, including developing reports, speeches, and articles; participating in stakeholder meetings; assisting in the development of information and policy guidance; and providing direct operational assistance to crime victim organizations, as appropriate.

Program Name Children's Justice Act Partnerships for Indian Communities Grant Program
FY 2012 Funding $2,700,000
OJP Sponsor OVC
Web Link www.ovc.gov
Program Contact Tanya Miller, (202) 616-3453, Tanya.Miller4@usdoj.gov
Program Description
The Children's Justice Act Partnerships for Indian Communities Grant Program is designed to support demonstration projects in American Indian/Alaska Native communities that improve the investigation, prosecution, and case management of child abuse, sexual abuse and physical abuse cases, in a manner that increases support for and lessens trauma to child abuse victims. Grantees awarded through this program will receive training and technical assistance to support program implementation.

Program Name Sexual Assault Forensic Medical Examination Telemedicine Center: An Innovative Pilot Project
FY 2012 Funding $3,500,000
OJP Sponsor OVC /NIJ
Web Link www.ovc.gov
Program Contacts Marnie Shiels, (202) 616-3609, marnie.shiels2@usdoj.gov; Ivette Estrada, (202) 307-0932, Ivette.estrada@usdoj.gov
Program Description
Research has demonstrated that Sexual Assault Nurse Examiner (SANE) programs and Sexual Assault Response Teams (SART) are effective at enhancing the quality of health care for sexual assault victims, improving the quality of forensic evidence collected, and increasing prosecution rates over time; however, for rural and tribal areas, it can be difficult to start SANE and SART programs due to a lack of resources. In addition, it can be difficult for medical personnel to get sufficient experience due to the small number of exams performed. The purpose of this project is to provide live access to SANEs, or other expert medical forensic examiners, for four pilot sites that will be selected through a separate solicitation issued by the recipient of this award in partnership with the Office for Victims of Crime (OVC). Sites may include rural, tribal, military, urban/suburban without a current medical forensic program, and/or correctional settings. The recipient will be expected to create a national telemedicine center for sexual assault medical forensic exams. The center should be staffed 24 hours a day, 7 days a week, with highly trained,

experienced SANEs or SAFEs. The telemedicine center must have the technological capability for the individuals to directly assist in the examinations being conducted at the pilot sites. The award recipient will also be expected to carry out a process evaluation of the project.

Training and Technical Assistance

Program Name Training and Technical Assistance to Improve Understanding and Application of Research and Evaluation in Victim Services
FY 2012 Funding $250,000
OJP Sponsor OVC
Web Link www.ovc.gov
Program Contact Meg Morrow (202) 307-5983, Meg.Morrow@usdoj.gov
Program Description
Under this project, OVC will support a national initiative to assist the field in becoming more educated contributors to and consumers of research and evaluation that can lead to more effective and cost-efficient services for victims of crime. The grantee will develop training and technical assistance that can be delivered through interactive online access.

Program Name National Field Generated Demonstration Projects Responding to Poly-Victimization Issues
FY 2012 Funding $1,500,000
OJP Sponsor OVC
Web Link www.ovc.gov
Program Contact Sharron Chapman, (202) 305-2358, Sharron.Chapman@usdoj.gov
Program Description
This program improves the capacity of crime victim service organizations and partners to advance victims' rights and improve victims' services, with a focus on poly-victimization. The purpose of this effort is to fund the development of demonstration projects developed from a promising practice, model, or program to identify and address awareness and service needs of victims who suffer from poly-victimization.

Program Name American Indian and Alaska Native Training and Technical Assistance (TTA) Program
FY 2012 Funding $750,000
OJP Sponsor OVC
Web Link www.ovc.gov
Program Contact Kathleen Gless, (202) 307-6049, Kathleen.Gless@usdoj.gov; Tanya Miller, (202) 307-3453, Tanya.Miller4@usdoj.gov
Program Description
Through this program, OVC will support a TTA provider who demonstrates recognition of and experience with the importance of culture, history, traditions, and spirituality inherent in the American Indian and Alaska Native (AI/AN) community, as well as the value of adapting community and evidence-based victim assistance intervention strategies for tribal communities. The OVC AI&AN TTA Program will support OVC's Children's Justice Act (CJA) Partnerships for Indian Communities and Comprehensive Tribal Victim Assistance (CTVAP) sites. The purpose of the program is to support and enhance the CJA and CTVAP sites' capacity to coordinate and provide a comprehensive array of culturally and linguistically appropriate services to victims of crime, their families, and the community. The TTA provider will be expected to develop an appropriate approach for each site. The TTA provider will help sites conduct comprehensive community needs assessments; develop strategic plans; and implement tools and mechanisms for collecting data for performance measures and program evaluation that will enhance and build sustainable, culturally relevant, comprehensive victim-centered CJA or CTVAP projects.

Program Name State Victim Assistance Academy (SVAA) New
FY 2012 Funding $210,000
OJP Sponsor OVC
Web Link www.ovc.gov
Program Contact Richard Greenough, (202) 616-8715, Richard.greenough2@usdoj.gov
Program Description

This program will provide $35,000 grants to support up to six states in phase one of the establishment of a State Victim Assistance Academy (SVAA). SVAAs provide training to develop skills of victim assistance providers from community- and systems-based programs. Applicants are limited to the states that do not have an SVAA funded by OVC. For more information on where OVC-funded SVAAs are located, visit www.ovc.gov/assist/existingsvaa.html. Applicants are limited to public agencies, colleges and universities, state governments, and private nonprofit organizations, including faith-based organizations that can demonstrate capability to carry out all statewide planning activities required by the funded project. Two states may jointly apply for funding to develop a regional SVAA.

Research and Statistical Programs

Program Name Supplementary Study of Victimization of People with Disabilities in Institutional Settings
FY 2012 Funding OVC $500,000; BJS $1,500,000
OJP Sponsor BJS/OVC
Web Link www.ovc.gov; bjs.ojp.usdoj.gov
Program Contact BJS William Sabol, (202) 514-1062, William.Sabol@usdoj.gov;
OVC Jasmine D'Addario-Fobian, (202) 305-3332, jasmine.d'addario-fobian@usdoj.gov
Program Description
Limited statistical information exists about crime victims with disabilities, especially those in institutions. The National Crime Victimization Survey is not adequate to capture information about this population. BJS has partnered with OVC to pursue, through a competitive solicitation, research both to supplement and complement the general information currently available. Information obtained ideally would be able to be extrapolated across populations and will illustrate the Justice Department's seriousness and commitment to addressing the issues of crime victims with disabilities.

Program Name Methodological Research To Support the Redesign of the National Crime Victimization Survey (NCVS)
FY 2012 Funding TBD
OJP Sponsor BJS
Web Link bjs.ojp.usdoj.gov
Program Contact William Sabol, (202) 514-1062, William.Sabol@usdoj.gov
Program Description
The purpose of the project is to implement a pilot test for boosting the NCVS sample in a set of states to test the feasibility of state boosts for the national design of the NCVS. This test will move the NCVS towards its goals related to subnational estimates of criminal victimization, improve survey methodology, and introduce sample allocation methods that can provide for long-term economies of scale associated with producing state-level estimates of criminal victimization. It also will better meet the challenges of measuring the extent, characteristics, and consequences of criminal victimization as it exists today or may evolve in the future.

Program Name NCVS Victim/Offender Overlap and Victimization
FY 2012 Funding $1,000,000
OJP Sponsor BJS
Web Link bjs.ojp.usdoj.gov
Program Contact William Sabol, (202) 514-1062, William.Sabol@usdoj.gov
Program Description

This project will involve the design and testing of instruments to measure the victimization and offending experiences among a sample of jail inmates. The focus of the project will be on instrumentation that measures both prior victimization and offense behavior. Testing of the instrument will occur among a sample of jail inmates. This design work will inform BJS efforts to field a national implementation of a jail inmate survey that samples from the flow of inmates arriving into jails after booking to generate estimates of victimization rates (prior to jail admission) of hard-to-measure populations (such as homeless persons and highly mobile persons) in order to better understand the victim/offender overlap.

Program Name Research and Evaluation on Violence Against Women: Sexual Violence, Stalking, and Teen Dating Violence
FY 2012 Funding $3,000,000
OJP Sponsor NIJ
Web Link www.nij.gov/funding/welcome.htm
Program Contact Bethany Backes, (202) 305-4419,Bethany.Backes@usdoj.gov or Carrie Mulford, (202) 307-2959, Carrie.Mulford@usdoj.gov
Program Description
NIJ is seeking research and evaluation on specific issues related to sexual violence, stalking, and teen dating violence. The issue areas for sexual violence research are the criminal justice response to particular underserved populations; the development and testing of instruments with diverse populations; and testing of innovative interventions aimed at improving initial criminal justice responses to victims of sexual violence. Priority areas for research on stalking are evaluating offender interventions specific to stalking behavior by current or former intimate partners; and law enforcement and prosecutorial actions regarding particular stalking issues. In the area of teen dating violence (i.e. adolescent relationship abuse), applications are sought for additional waves of data for existing longitudinal projects.

Program Name Longitudinal Data on Teen Dating Violence: Postdoctoral Fellowship
FY 2012 Funding $600,000
OJP Sponsor NIJ
Web Link www.nij.gov/funding/welcome.htm
Program Contact Carrie Mulford, (202) 307-2959, Carrie.Mulford@usdoj.gov
Program Description
NIJ is seeking applications for research related to teen dating violence (i.e. adolescent relationship abuse). In particular, NIJ is seeking proposals that explore predictors and consequences of teen dating violence using longitudinal data through the support of postdoctoral fellows to analyze existing data.

Program Name Replication Research on Sexual Violence Case Attrition
FY 2012 Funding $1,200,000
OJP Sponsor NIJ
Web Link www.nij.gov/funding/welcome.htm
Program Contact Bethany Backes, (202) 305-4419, Bethany.Backes@usdoj.gov
Program Description
NIJ seeks proposals for funding for one research grant to replicate the study "Police Decision Making in Sexual Assault Cases: An Analysis of Crimes Reported to the Los Angeles Police Department, 2006-2008" (NIJ Grant # 2009-WG-BX-0009) at six sites. Sites should cover urban, suburban, and rural areas. Proposals should, to the extent possible, replicate the mixed methods design and analytic approach as found in the final technical report and data documentation files of the aforementioned study.

Program Name Violent Victimization Among Racial and Ethnic Minorities
FY 2012 Funding $750,000
OJP Sponsor NIJ
Web Link www.nij.gov/funding/welcome.htm
Program Contact Nadine Frederique, (202) 514-8777, Nadine.Frederique@usdoj.gov
Program Description

NIJ seeks proposals for funding for a study that constitutes new research on the violent victimization experiences of racial and ethnic minority males and/or females. NIJ seeks to move this body of research forward by examining the breadth of causes of differential victimization rates among racial and ethnic minorities.

Program Name Research on the Link between Victimization and Offending
FY 2012 Funding $750,000
OJP Sponsor NIJ
Web Link www.nij.gov/funding/welcome.htm
Program Contact Dara Blachman-Demner, (202) 514-9528, Dara.Blachman-Demner@usdoj.gov or Carrie Mulford, (202) 307-2959, Carrie.Mulford@usdoj.gov
Program Description
NIJ seeks proposals to conduct research that enhances knowledge of the relationship between victimization and offending, with an emphasis on criminal incidents or events. NIJ encourages applicants to submit proposals for bold, innovative approaches to enhancing the current understanding of the processes linking criminal offending and victimization.

Program Name Evaluability Assessments of the Circles of Support and Accountability Model
FY 2012 Funding $125,000
OJP Sponsor NIJ
Web Link www.nij.gov/funding/welcome.htm
Program Contact Marie Garcia, (202) 514–7128, Marie.Garcia@usdoj.gov
Program Description
As part of a collaborative effort with the Office of Sex Offender Sentencing, Monitoring, Apprehending, Registering, and Tracking (SMART), NIJ seeks competitive proposals for a single award that will support an evaluability assessment of up to five sites that are implementing the Circles of Support and Accountability (COSA) model. Results from the evaluability assessments may become a precursor to further research and program development work, lay possible groundwork for other targeted research, and assist with the coordination of extramural and intramural research and evaluation efforts sponsored by NIJ and partnering agencies (e.g., the SMART Office").

Section 6

Enhancing Law Enforcement Initiatives

Overview

Community partnerships have contributed to the decline in violent crime in many U.S. cities. However, sections in some cities, as well as in some small towns and rural areas, continue to be plagued by high instances of violent crime. OJP will continue to work closely with state, local, and tribal law enforcement organizations, researchers, and other professionals to develop and implement strategies to address the needs of these locales.

In addition, OJP recognizes that the nation's economic issues require close examination of federal, state, and local spending. Public leaders are reallocating resources to optimize the return on public investment. Due to budgetary constraints, law enforcement leaders need to examine and adopt evidence-based and data-driven strategies for crime reduction efforts.

The grant programs outlined in this chapter are intended to help state, local, and tribal law enforcement and other partners respond to constrained budgets and still ensure public safety.

Discretionary Programs

Program Name Adam Walsh Act (AWA) Implementation Grant Program
FY 2012 Funding $12,800,000
OJP Sponsor SMART Office
Web Link www.smart.gov
Program Contact Victoria Jolicoeur, (202) 514-4696, Victoria.Jolicoeur@usdoj.gov
Program Description
The Support for Adam Walsh Act (AWA) Implementation Grant Program assists jurisdictions with developing and/or enhancing programs designed to implement requirements of the Sex Offender Notification and Registration Act (SORNA) and to promote innovation and best practices in the field of sex offender management. In summary, SORNA requires that all states, the District of Columbia, the principal U.S. territories, and participating federally recognized Indian tribes maintain a sex offender registry; and that sex offenders register and maintain a current registration in each jurisdiction where the offender resides, is an employee, or is a student. SORNA also sets forth requirements for sex offender registries, which include specified required information; duration of registration; in-person verification of sex offender identity; and participation in the Dru Sjodin National Sex Offender Public Website, and the utilization of the SORNA Exchange Portal.

Activities supported by this program may include the following:

- developing or enhancing jurisdiction-wide SORNA implementation programs or functions;
- enhancing infrastructure to assist implementation of SORNA, such as for the collection, storage, submission or analysis of sex offender biometric data (finger and palm prints) and DNA;
- developing or enhancing law enforcement and other criminal justice agency information sharing at the jurisdiction level, as well as between jurisdiction level agencies and local level agencies as it relates to SORNA implementation;
- implementing records management projects, such as converting documents to digital format as required by SORNA;
- providing support for coordinated interagency efforts to enhance implementation of SORNA requirements;
- supporting efforts of local or state units of government (including P.L. 280 tribes) to develop or enhance their sex offender registration and notification functions with tribal

nations as delegated to the state for the purpose of substantial implementation of SORNA; and

- developing and implementing training for law enforcement and other criminal justice agency personnel responsible for sex offender registration, notification, and monitoring as it relates to SORNA implementation in the jurisdiction.

Program Name Enhanced Collaborative Model to Combat Human Trafficking
FY 2012 Funding $3,727,327
OJP Sponsor BJA
Web Link www.bja.gov/funding.aspx
Program Contact Deborah Meader, (202) 305-2601, Deborah.Meader@usdoj.gov
Program Description
Human trafficking is reputed to be one of the most profitable and fastest growing endeavors of organized crime—an endeavor that enslaves thousands of people within the United States each year and perhaps millions internationally. The DOJ includes investigating human trafficking among its top priorities. To address this problem, BJA will continue to provide funds for state, local, and tribal law enforcement to proactively investigate human trafficking with the primary goal of identifying and rescuing victims of severe forms of trafficking. These are defined as: (1) sex trafficking in which a commercial sex act is induced by force, fraud, or coercion, or in which the person induced to perform such an act has not attained 18 years of age; or (2) the recruitment, harboring, transportation, provision, or obtaining of a person for labor or services through the use of force, fraud, or coercion for the purpose of subjection to involuntary servitude, peonage, debt bondage, or slavery.

Program Name Bulletproof Vest Partnership (BVP)
Grantee Any recognized unit of general government recognized by the U.S. Census Bureau that employs law enforcement officers.
FY 2012 Funding $20,072,197
OJP Sponsor BJA
Web Link www.ojp.usdoj.gov/bvpbasi/
Program Contact Joe Husted, (202) 353-4411, Joseph.Husted@usdoj.gov
Program Description
This program reimburses states and local units of government up to 50 percent of the cost of a bulletproof vest for a law enforcement officer. The application opens once a year, but payments are made year round in monthly batches and are usable for a two-year period. Once a jurisdiction receives an award, it must request funds and provide vest receipts.

Program Name Protecting Public Health, Safety, and the Economy from Counterfeit Goods and Product Piracy: The Intellectual Property Theft Enforcement Program
FY 2012 Funding $2,200,000
OJP Sponsor BJA
Web Link www.bja.gov/funding.aspx
Program Contact Kate McNamee, (202) 514-9343, Catherine.McNamee@usdoj.gov
Program Description
The Intellectual Property Theft Enforcement Program is designed to provide national support and improve the capacity of state, local, and tribal criminal justice systems to address intellectual property criminal enforcement, including prosecution, prevention, training, and technical assistance.

Program Name Violent Gang and Gun Crime Reduction Program Project Safe Neighborhoods (PSN) Grant Program
FY 2012 Funding $521,777
OJP Sponsor BJA
Web Link www.bja.gov/ProgramDetails.aspx?Program_ID=74
Program Contact James Chavis, (202) 307-0688, James.Chavis@usdoj.gov
Program Description

Project Safe Neighborhoods (PSN) is designed to create safer neighborhoods through a sustained reduction in crime associated with gang and gun violence. The program's effectiveness is based on the cooperation of local, state, and federal agencies engaged in a unified approach led by the U.S. Attorney (USA). The USA is responsible for establishing a collaborative PSN task force of federal, state, and local law enforcement and other community members to implement gang and gun crime enforcement, intervention and prevention initiatives within the district. Through the PSN task force, the USA will implement the five design features of PSN—partnerships, strategic planning, training, outreach, and accountability—to address specific gun and gang crime problems in that district.

Program Name National Criminal History Improvement Program (NCHIP)
FY 2012 Funding $6,000,000
OJP Sponsor BJS
Web Link bjs.ojp.usdoj.gov
Program Contact Devon B. Adams, (202) 514-9157, Devon.Adams@usdoj.gov
Program Description
The NCHIP program helps states, territories, and tribes to improve the quality, timeliness, and immediate accessibility of criminal history and related records for use by federal, state, local, and tribal law enforcement. These records play a vital role in supporting criminal investigations, background checks, and efforts to enforce protective orders issued in response to stalking and domestic violence offenses. Funds awarded support the following goals: (1) Improving the completeness, accuracy, and timeliness of criminal history records and related records, including those that are related to protection orders, stalking, domestic violence, and prohibiting mental health records; (2) upgrading the technology and equipment supporting national and state criminal history records systems; and (3) assisting states in fully implementing the National Crime Prevention and Privacy Compact, which governs the interstate exchange of criminal records for non-criminal-justice purposes.

Program Name National Instant Criminal Background Check System(NICS) Act Record Improvement Program (NARIP)
FY 2012 Funding $5,000,000
OJP Sponsor BJS
Web Link bjs.ojp.usdoj.gov
Program Contact Devon B. Adams, (202) 514-9157, Devon.Adams@usdoj.gov
Program Description
The NICS Act Record Improvement Program is a product of the enactment of the NICS Improvement Amendments Act of 2007, which contains a number of provisions aimed at improving the NICS, established by the FBI pursuant to the Brady Handgun Violence Prevention Act to support conducting criminal background checks for regulated firearm purchases. The program helps states and tribal governments make records available to the NICS relating to persons who are disqualified from possessing or receiving a firearm. Among other objectives, grants can be used to establish or upgrade information and identification technologies for firearms eligibility determinations, and to improve the automation and transmittal of criminal history dispositions and records and mental health adjudications or commitments to federal and state record repositories.

Training and Technical Assistance

Program Name Anti-Human Trafficking Task Force Initiative Training and Technical Assistance
FY 2012 Funding $305,000
OJP Sponsor BJA
Web Link www.bja.gov/funding.aspx
Program Contact Deborah Meader, (202) 305-2601, Deborah.Meader@usdoj.gov
Program Description
BJA and OVC work collaboratively to utilize funds appropriated through the Trafficking Victims Protection Act (TVPA) to implement a multidisciplinary anti-human trafficking task force model

designed to combat human trafficking by identifying, rescuing, and restoring victims (with a focus on foreign national victims); investigating and prosecuting trafficking crimes; and raising awareness about trafficking in the surrounding community. TTA funds will be used to continue supporting comprehensive training and technical assistance to the BJA-funded task forces and OVC-funded victim service providers.

Program Name Missing Alzheimer's Program
FY 2012 Funding $893,842
OJP Sponsor BJA
Web Link www.bja.gov
Program Contact Linda Hammond-Deckard, (202) 514-6015 , Linda.Hammond-Deckard@usdoj.gov
Program Description
The Missing Alzheimer's Program provides funds for projects that aid in the protection and location of missing persons living with Alzheimer's disease and related dementias, and other missing elderly individuals.

Research and Statistical Programs

Program Name National Use of Force Data Collection Design
FY 2012 Funding $75,000
OJP Sponsor BJS
Web Link bjs.ojp.usdoj.gov
Program Contact Joel Garner, (202) 305-2682, Joel.Garner@usdoj.gov
Program Description
This program seeks proposals for the design of a statistical program that will generate estimates of the nature and extent of the use of lethal and nonlethal force by law enforcement officers in the United States. This design program will systematically assess the strengths and weaknesses of measurement strategies, sampling frames, and analytical approaches used in prior research and statistical programs on uses of force. This assessment will identify promising approaches for inclusion in a BJS use-of-force program, and test the extent to which it is feasible to implement these promising strategies, frames, and approaches in an efficient and cost effective manner.

Program Name Census of Law Enforcement Training Academies, 2012
FY 2012 Funding $318,500
OJP Sponsor BJS
Web Link bjs.ojp.usdoj.gov
Program Contact Joel Garner, (202) 305-2682, Joel.Garner@usdoj.gov
Program Description
This program seeks proposals for a census of law enforcement training academies. Such academies are designed to provide new law enforcement recruits with the knowledge, skills, and values essential to successfully implementing contemporary laws, policies, and procedures into police work. The structure, personnel and curriculum of these academies vary greatly in response to local preferences, state laws, liability suits, and emerging trends in police practices. In addition to organizational characteristics of the training academies, this census will collect information on the number and types of officers trained; content and length of the training program; hours of instruction on each topic in the training curriculum; number and type of instructors; requirements for instructors; on-site and off-site training facilities; operating budget; and retention rates by race and gender.

Program Name Research on Policing
FY 2012 Funding $1,000,000
OJP Sponsor NIJ
Web Link www.nij.gov/funding/welcome.htm

Program Contact Brett Chapman, (202) 514-2187, Brett.Chapman@usdoj.gov or Eric D. Martin, (202) 514-9588, Eric.D.Martin@usdoj.gov

Program Description

NIJ seeks proposals to conduct research on policing to improve criminal investigative processes and promote police integrity in law enforcement agencies at the state and local levels. NIJ intends to extend the previous line of research with a study on the criminal investigation process, with an emphasis on changes and/or improvements in the investigative processes over the past thirty years. Additionally, NIJ is interested in changes in investigative processes that have resulted in different models of investigations, and changes in detectives' investigative practices in the direction of crime control and prevention.

Program Name Census of State and Local Law Enforcement Agencies
FY 2012 Funding $700,000
OJP Sponsor BJS
Web Link bjs.ojp.usdoj.gov
Program Contact Joel Garner, (202) 305-2682, Joel.Garner@usdoj.gov
Program Description
Description This program seeks proposals to implement a census of law enforcement agencies in the United States. The census will provide national data on the number of state and local law enforcement agencies and employees for local police departments, sheriffs' offices, state law enforcement agencies, and special jurisdiction agencies, such as campus, housing, natural resources, and other specialized agencies. This census serves as the sampling frame for other surveys of law enforcement agencies conducted by BJS and other agencies.

Program Name Criminal, Civil, and Regulatory Responses to White Collar Crime Program
FY 2012 Funding $1,200,000
OJP Sponsor BJS
Web Link bjs.ojp.usdoj.gov
Program Contact Howard Snyder, (202) 616-8305, Howard.Snyder@usdoj.gov
Program Description The federal response to white-collar violations is divided among criminal, civil, and regulatory justice agencies. Administrative data exist, but are currently not linked in a fashion that would provide counts of reported white-collar violations across federal agencies; the sanctions imposed (civil forfeiture, injunctions, cease-and-desist orders, fines, imprisonment), and the business sectors most vulnerable to financial crimes. The proposed project would draw on the recommendations made by Reiss and Biderman (1980) to reconcile differences in classification, definition, and counting from existing criminal, civil, and regulatory justice agencies (SEC, FTC, FDA, EPA, etc.) to provide a comprehensive and standardized reporting system of financial/economic crimes.

Program Name: Research on Illegal Prescription Drug Market Interventions
FY 2012 Funding: up to $1,000,000
OJP Sponsor: NIJ
Web Link www.nij.gov/funding/welcome.htm
Program Contacts Linda Truitt, (202) 353-9081, Linda.Truitt@usdoj.gov; Alan Spanbauer, (202) 305-2436, Alan.Spanbuer@usdoj.gov, and William Ford, (202) 353-9768, William.Ford@usdoj.gov.
Program Description
Up to $2 million may become available for multiple research grants on illegal prescription drug markets to examine the utility of policies, practices, and resources available to law enforcement for major crime deterrence, prosecution, and other market intervention measures. This solicitation has two objectives: policy analysis of criminal diversion of prescription medication laws; and Prescription Drug Monitoring Program (PDMP) optimization for law enforcement. It seeks to determine the effectiveness of federal and state criminal diversion of prescription medication laws that establish definitions and punishments intended to target "rogue pain clinics," illegal Internet pharmacies, drug theft, illicit prescribing by physicians, and doctor shopping; to establish the utility of PDMP information to law enforcement, including prosecutors

and task forces; and to discover how states can optimize the quality and flow of this sensitive information.

Program Name The Impact of Different Safety Equipment Modalities on Reducing Correctional Officer Injuries
FY 2012 Funding $400,000
OJP Sponsor NIJ
Web Link www.nij.gov/funding/welcome.htm
Program Contact Jack Harne, (202) 616-2911, Jack.Harne@usdoj.gov
Program Description
With this solicitation, NIJ seeks proposals to conduct comparative evaluations of safety equipment modalities: policies and practices among correctional agencies regarding what safety equipment staff may use, when and how staff use it, and how those modalities affect officers' physical safety. This solicitation defines safety equipment as equipment used by correctional officers to de-escalate and stop violent and disruptive activities by inmates and to protect officers from assaults.

Program Name Evaluability Assessment of Law Enforcement Agencies Using the Data-Driven Approaches to Crime and Traffic Safety
FY 2012 Funding $300,000 (from Department of Transportation)
OJP Sponsor NIJ
Web Link www.nij.gov/nij/funding/forthcoming.htm
Program Contact Brett Chapman, (202) 514-2187, Brett.Chapman@usdoj.gov, Joel Hunt, 202-616-8111, Joel.Hunt@usdoj.gov, or Eric D. Martin, (202) 514-9588, Eric.D.Martin@usdoj.gov
Program Description
NIJ, through an Interagency Agreement with the National Highway Traffic Safety Administration (NHTSA) is interested in determining the feasibility of conducting a rigorous evaluation of the DDACTS process. NIJ seeks to fund an evaluability assessment of up to 15 law enforcement agencies currently employing the DDACTS model. Approximately 250 law enforcement agencies have been encouraged to adopt the guiding principles of the DDACTS model in their law enforcement strategies.

Program Name Research and Evaluation on Metropolitan Crime
FY 2012 Funding $750,000
OJP Sponsor NIJ
Web Link www.nij.gov/nij/funding/forthcoming.htm
Program Contact Brett Chapman, (202) 514-2187, Brett.Chapman@usdoj.gov, Joel Hunt, 202-616-8111, Joel.Hunt@usdoj.gov, or Eric D. Martin, (202)514-9588, Eric.D.Martin@usdoj.gov
Program Description
NIJ is interested in funding criminal justice research that leverages municipal operation datasets both within and across jurisdictions. NIJ is interested in the feasibility of combining multiple datasets from various agencies to conduct research on criminal justice issues in urban and suburban environments. This research is critical in enhancing public safety by giving law enforcement the tools to understand the changing nature of crime in metropolitan areas.

Program Name: "NIJ Body Armor Challenge"
FY2012 Funding: $100,000
OJP Sponsor NIJ
Web Link http://www.nij.gov
Program Contact Mark Greene, (202) 307-3384, mark.greene@ojp.usdoj.gov
Program Description
NIJ seeks viable solutions to determine the ballistic performance of individual in-service body armor at any point in time to a high degree of accuracy, and in a manner that does not render the armor unfit for continued use. To be released as a technology challenge on www.challenge.gov

Section 7

Supporting Innovation in Adjudication

Overview

Increasing fairness and public trust in the justice system is an OJP priority. Special efforts must be made to address challenging and diverse problems throughout the court system. Through investments in innovative initiatives such as problem-solving courts, effective case flow management, community prosecution, indigent defense, and reentry efforts, OJP has helped jurisdictions realize measurable gains in public trust, while also increasing capacity and reducing crime.

OJP's integrated approach to justice reform engages the community and promotes multidisciplinary collaboration and training on issues that advance public safety. This approach, especially with regard to policy decisions and resource allocation, ensures that communities are able effectively to utilize a limited pool of available resources to address social and economic issues related to incarceration. While local court personnel will decide how to meet the community's specific needs, OJP is committed to providing the resources, tools, and support to help them test their ideas.

Adjudication programs and initiatives address each phase of the criminal justice cycle, from pretrial risk assessments and pre-adjudication diversion initiatives to community-oriented justice to effectively addressing reentry. These efforts are aimed at shifting the policy-making paradigm towards community-strengthening investments instead of increased incarceration. Through close partnerships with stakeholders and national organizations, OJP supports jurisdictions with training and technical assistance, enabling them to address inefficiencies in their programs during various stages of the adjudication process. OJP also relies on field practitioners to provide valuable insight on developing targeted, sustainable solutions nationwide.

In addition to the initiatives listed in this chapter, OJP is addressing training and technical assistance needs for indigent defense; providing training and technical assistance for criminal courts to improve their management and operations; and providing training on the "*CSI* effect" and other issues surrounding juror bias. As we look forward, OJP will target emerging issues that courts need to address, including the increasing numbers of senior citizens in the court process, mortgage fraud, and racial disparities in the criminal justice system.

Discretionary Programs

Program Name Wrongful Conviction Review Program
FY 2012 Funding $687,525
OJP Sponsor BJA
Web Link www.bja.gov/funding.aspx
Program Contact Catherine McNamee, (202) 514-9343, Catherine.McNamee@usdoj.gov
Program Description
The Wrongful Conviction Review Program seeks to provide high quality representation for defendants with post-conviction claims of innocence. Post-conviction innocence claims are likely to include complex challenges to the reliability and accuracy of evidence presented at trial. Problematic evidence falls into three categories—eyewitness identification evidence, confession evidence, and forensic evidence. In some cases, post-conviction DNA testing alone can prove innocence, but the majority of cases require other, more costly forms of proof, including DNA testing and expert testimony. The goals of this initiative are to provide quality representation to the wrongfully convicted; to alleviate burdens placed on the criminal justice system through costly and prolonged post-conviction litigation; and to identify, when possible, the actual perpetrator of the crime.

Program Name Southwest Border Prosecution Initiative (SWBPI)
FY 2012 Funding $8,988,415 (includes NBPI, below)
OJP Sponsor BJA
Web Link www.ojp.usdoj.gov/swbpi/index.html
Program Contact Joe Husted, (202) 353-4411, Joseph.Husted@usdoj.gov
Program Description
This initiative provides funds to eligible jurisdictions in the four southwest border states (Arizona, California, New Mexico, and Texas) for qualifying federally initiated and declined-referred criminal cases that were disposed of after October 1, 2005. Successful applicants may use their federal funds for any lawful purpose. A federally initiated and referred criminal case is eligible if it was prosecuted by a state or county prosecutor and disposed of during one of the eligibility periods. Jurisdictions providing pretrial detention for eligible case defendants are also eligible for funds. Federally referred cases that are declined and not prosecuted by state or county prosecutors are ineligible. Jurisdictions participating in the State Criminal Alien Assistance Program are permitted to apply.

Program Name Northern Border Prosecution Initiative (NBPI)
FY 2012 Funding $8,988,415 (includes SWBPI, above)
OJP Sponsor BJA
Web Link www.ojp.usdoj.gov/nbpi/
Program Contact Joe Husted, (202) 353-4411, Joseph.Husted@usdoj.gov
Program Description This initiative provides funds to eligible jurisdictions in the 14 northern border states (Alaska, Idaho, Maine, Michigan, Minnesota, Montana, New Hampshire, New York, North Dakota, Ohio, Pennsylvania, Vermont, Washington, and Wisconsin) for qualifying federally initiated and declined-referred criminal cases that were disposed of after October 1, 2005. Although reimbursements from NBPI federal payments may be used by applicant jurisdictions for any purpose not otherwise prohibited by federal law, using funds to support and enhance additional prosecutorial and detention services is encouraged. A federally initiated and referred criminal case is eligible if it was prosecuted by a state or county prosecutor and disposed of during one of the eligibility periods. Jurisdictions providing pretrial detention for eligible case defendants are also eligible for funds. Federally referred cases that are declined and not prosecuted by state or county prosecutors are ineligible. Jurisdictions participating in the State Criminal Alien Assistance Program are permitted to apply.

Training and Technical Assistance

Program Name Capital Case Litigation Initiative (CCLI)
FY 2012 Funding $2,000,000
OJP Sponsor BJA
Web Link www.bja.gov/funding.aspx
Program Contact Alissa Huntoon, (202) 305-1661, Alissa.Huntoon@usdoj.gov
Program Description
This initiative is designed to provide high quality training and technical assistance on death penalty issues to judges, defense attorneys, and prosecutors. Program goals are to increase the number of court officials trained in capital case procedures and strategies and to ensure that defense attorneys and prosecutors have the most up-to-date and comprehensive information available on death penalty litigation. BJA will continue to improve the quality of capital case litigation training by requiring states to utilize curricula that have been developed and piloted specifically for prosecutors and defense attorneys.

Program Name Tribal Criminal and Civil Legal Assistance (TCCLA)
FY 2012 Funding $2,250,000
OJP Sponsor BJA
Web Link: www.bja.gov/funding.aspx
Program Contact Norena Henry, (202) 616-3205, Norena.henry@usdoj.gov
Program Description

The TCCLA program helps enhance the operations of tribal justice systems and improves access to those systems. TCCLA provides grants to organizations to provide legal services for indigent defendants and respondents in tribal justice systems. In addition, this solicitation calls for applications to provide training and technical assistance for the development, enrichment, and enhancement of judicial system personnel and practices within tribal justice systems. Eligible organizations for direct service grants are tribal and non-tribal non-profit (Internal Revenue Code (I.R.C.) § 501(c)(3)) entities, including tribal enterprises and educational institutions (public, private and tribal colleges and universities), that provide legal assistance services for federally recognized Indian tribes; members of federally recognized Indian tribes; or tribal justice systems pursuant to federal poverty guidelines. Eligible organizations for the training and technical assistance grants are national or regional membership organizations and associations whose membership or membership section consists of judicial system personnel within tribal justice systems.

Research and Statistical Programs

Program Name National Pretrial Reporting Program
FY 2011 Funding $250,000
OJP Sponsor BJS
Web Link bjs.ojp.usdoj.gov
Program Contact Howard Snyder, (202) 616-8305, Howard.Snyder@usdoj.gov
Program Description Traditionally, BJS has collected pretrial data at the state court level through the State Court Processing Statistics (SCPS) program. SCPS, however, has several key limitations including the fact that it does not obtain data on several key pretrial elements and is limited to felony case processing in the nation's 75 most populous counties. The National Pretrial Reporting Program (NPRP) will attempt to expand BJS' pretrial research capacity by examining the methods in which defendants can be released or detained in state trial courts. It will aim to identify the types of pretrial release methods (e.g., surety bond, pretrial diversion programs, and release on recognizance) utilized in all 3,100 counties and ascertain the availability of obtaining specific pretrial data for each surveyed county. The work would explore appropriate data sources such as courts, pretrial service agencies, pretrial supervision organizations, and other relevant entities in an effort to develop a nationally representative framework for tracking defendants released through various pretrial mechanisms in state courts.

Program Name Social Science Research on Indigent Defense
FY 2012 Funding $1,000,000
OJP Sponsor NIJ
Web Link www.nij.gov/funding/welcome.htm
Program Contact Nadine Frederique, (202) 514-8777, Nadine.Frederique@usdoj.gov or Donna Davis (202 514-9331, Donna.Davis@usdoj.gov
Program Description
NIJ seeks to fund research that can help with understanding the barriers faced by indigent criminal defendants to securing legal representation; offering recommendations to address these barriers; and disseminating the recommendations in a practical and easily accessible manner to practitioners across the United States.

Section 8

Advancing Technology to Prevent and Solve Crime

Overview

Criminal justice practitioners require new and improved technologies to protect the public; ensure officer safety; confirm the guilty and protect the innocent; improve the efficiency of justice; and make informed decisions. Performance standards and compliance testing are critical pieces of the technology portfolio that assess the safety and effectiveness of the equipment public safety agencies buy and use. NIJ executes a research, development, testing, and evaluation program for technology projects, which leads to the development of needed technology and establishment of standards and compliance testing.

OJP offers grants for basic research and development to create new technology and refine existing technology. Grants have produced advances in many areas, including sensors and surveillance, specifically better walk-through and handheld metal detectors; interoperability of public safety communications technologies, including compatible radio systems and other telecommunications resources; biometrics digital forensics, resulting in more sophisticated ways to capture evidence on electronic products (e.g., laptops and cell phones); and general forensics pertaining to pattern and impression evidence, fingerprints, and toxicology.

NIJ has the largest, most robust criminal justice technology research program in the United States in several areas, including geospatial and crime mapping technology for criminal justice applications; digital forensics; DNA forensics; and other forensic technologies. Examples of program activities include the following:

- forensic research that led to the development of "mini-STRs" (short tandem repeat, meaning any short, repeating DNA sequence) that can generate a DNA profile from aged, degraded, or damaged samples, such as skeletal remains, which have greatly expanded the power of DNA technology to identify the guilty, exonerate the innocent, and identify the missing;
- research and development funding that led to the body armor commonly used by law enforcement agencies today, which has been credited with saving more 3,000 lives over the past 20 years;
- research into the physiological effects of conducted energy devices (e.g., the TASER®), which have been shown to be safe and effective when used on healthy adults, and are very rarely associated with death of the subject; and
- a new initiative to combine data and crime mapping in such a way that law enforcement can "get in front of" the criminal instead of being reactive.

Over the next two years, OJP, NIJ, and their partners aim to develop enhanced data analytic tools for forecasting criminal trends and activities; improved hazardous protective equipment for criminal justice practitioners; better methods of protecting public venues from crime; and greater knowledge about the fundamental science underlying forensic science disciplines. They also will expand efforts to provide public safety practitioners with the means to deal with cell phones used for illicit purposes.

Discretionary Programs

Program Name Paul Coverdell Forensic Science Improvement Grants Program
FY 2012 Funding $10,586,098
OJP Sponsor NIJ
Web Link www.nij.gov/funding/welcome.htm

Program Contact Alan Spanbauer, (202) 305-2436, Alan.Spanbauer@usdoj.gov
Program Description
NIJ seeks proposals for the Paul Coverdell Forensic Science Improvement Grants Program, which awards grants to states and units of local government to help improve the quality and timeliness of forensic science and medical examiner services. Among other things, funds may be used to eliminate a backlog in the analysis of forensic evidence and to train and employ forensic laboratory personnel.

Program Name DNA Backlog Reduction Program
FY 2012 Funding $75,000,000
OJP Sponsor NIJ
Web Link www.nij.gov/funding/welcome.htm
Program Contact Mark Nelson, Senior Program Manager, (202) 616-1960, Mark.S.Nelson@usdoj.gov or Charles Heurich, (202) 616-9264, Charles.Heurich@usdoj.gov.
Program Description
The goal of NIJ's FY 2012 DNA Backlog Reduction Program is to assist eligible states and units of local government to process, record, screen, and analyze forensic DNA and/or DNA database samples; and to increase the capacity of public forensic DNA and DNA database laboratories to process more DNA samples, thereby reducing the number of forensic DNA and DNA database samples awaiting analysis.

Program Name Postconviction DNA Testing Assistance Program
FY 2012 Funding $3,545,366
OJP Sponsor NIJ
Web Link www.nij.gov/funding/welcome.htm
Program Contact Michael Dillon, (202) 514-5528, Michael.Dillon3@usdoj.gov.
Program Description
NIJ seeks proposals from states wishing to receive funding to help defray the costs associated with post conviction DNA testing in cases that involve violent felony offenses (as defined by state law) in which actual innocence might be demonstrated.

Program Name Solving Cold Cases with DNA
FY 2012 Funding $6,884,459
OJP Sponsor NIJ
Web Link www.nij.gov/funding/welcome.htm
Program Contact Charles Heurich, (202) 616-9264, Charles.Heurich@usdoj.gov
Program Description
NIJ will provide funding for states and units of local government to identify, review, and investigate violent crime cold cases that have the potential to be solved using DNA analysis, and to locate and analyze biological evidence associated with these cases. Experience has shown that cold case programs can solve a substantial number of violent crime cold cases, including homicides and sexual assaults. Advances in DNA technologies have substantially increased the successful DNA analysis of aged, degraded, limited, or otherwise compromised biological evidence. As a result, crime scene samples once thought to be unsuitable for testing may now yield DNA profiles. Additionally, samples that previously generated inconclusive DNA results may now be successfully analyzed using newer methods.

Research and Statistical Programs

Program Name Data Resources Program 2012 for the Analysis of Existing Data
FY 2012 Funding $240,000
OJP Sponsor NIJ
Web Link www.nij.gov/funding/welcome.htm
Program Contact Patrick Clark, (202) 353-9482, Patrick.clark@usdoj.gov
Program Description NIJ, BJS, and OJJDP have entered into a partnership with this Data Resources Program (DRP) solicitation to request applications for original research using existing

data available from the National Archive of Criminal Justice Data (NACJD) and other public sources.

Program Name Applied Research and Development in Forensic Science for Criminal Justice Purposes
FY 2012 Funding $8,000,000
OJP Sponsor NIJ
Web Link www.nij.gov/funding/welcome.htm
Program Contact Danielle McLeod-Henning, (202) 353-3812, Danielle.mcleod-henning@usdoj.gov
Program Description
With this solicitation, NIJ seeks proposals for applied research and development projects that will (1) increase knowledge or understanding necessary to guide forensic science policy and practice or (2) result in the production of useful materials, devices, systems, or methods that have the potential for forensic application. The intent of the program is to direct the findings of basic scientific research; research and development in broader scientific fields applicable to forensic science; and ongoing forensic science research, toward the development of highly discriminating, accurate, reliable, cost-effective, and rapid methods for the identification, analysis, and interpretation of physical evidence for criminal justice purposes.

Program Name Basic Scientific Research to Support Forensic Science for Criminal Justice Purposes
FY 2012 Funding $5,000,000
OJP Sponsor NIJ
Web Link www.nij.gov/funding/welcome.htm
Program Contact Danielle McLeod-Henning, (202) 353-3812, Danielle.mcleod-henning@usdoj.gov
Program Description
NIJ seeks proposals for funding basic scientific research in the physical, life, and cognitive sciences that is designed to increase the knowledge underlying forensic science disciplines intended for use in the criminal justice system.

Program Name Testing Geospatial Police Strategies and Exploring Their Relationship to Criminological Theories
FY 2012 Funding $500,000
OJP Sponsor NIJ
Web Link www.nij.gov/funding/welcome.htm
Program Contact Joel Hunt, (202) 616-8111, Joel.Hunt@usdoj.gov
Program Description
NIJ is seeking applications for research related to links among criminological theories and geospatial police strategies. In particular, NIJ is seeking proposals that test current geospatial police strategies implemented at the micro-place and micro-time levels.

Program Name Using DNA Technology to Identify the Missing
FY 2012 Funding $3,200,000
OJP Sponsor NIJ
Web Link www.nij.gov/funding/welcome.htm
Program Contact Charles Heurich, (202) 616-9264, Charles.Heurich@usdoj.gov
Program Description
NIJ seeks to provide funding to (1) assist eligible entities in performing DNA analysis on unidentified human remains and/or reference samples, to support the efforts of states and units of local government to identify missing persons; (2) enter the resulting DNA profiles into the FBI's National DNA Index System using the Combined DNA Index System (CODIS) version 7.0; and (3) enter any relevant case information related to unidentified remains into NamUs, as deemed appropriate by the submitting agency (if a case is not entered a justification will be required).

Program Name Evaluating the Impact of the NIJ Body Armor Program
FY 2012 Funding $400,000
OJP Sponsor NIJ
Web Link www.nij.gov/funding/welcome.htm
Program Contact Debra Stoe, (202) 616-7036, Debra.Stoe@usdoj.gov
Program Description
NIJ seeks proposals for funding to conduct an evaluation of the impact of NIJ's body armor research program on law enforcement policy and practice in the United States, from the program's inception in the early 1970s through today. This program involves the development of improved body armor, as well as the development of standards to measure the performance of body armor, and a testing program to help ensure that the armor sold to law enforcement agencies is safe and effective.

Program Name Research on the Impact of Technology on Policing Strategies in the 21st Century
FY 2012 Funding $1,000,000
OJP Sponsor NIJ
Web Link www.nij.gov/funding/welcome.htm
Program Contact Brett Chapman, (202) 514-2187, brett.chapman@usdoj.gov;
Eric Martin, (202) 514-9588, Eric.D.Martin@usdoj.gov
Program Description
NIJ seeks proposals to conduct research that evaluates how technology affects policing strategies at the state, local, and tribal levels, and the impact technology has on policing outcomes. Policing organizations today may implement new technologies within their departments for the purpose of promoting public safety, enforcing the law, and/or preventing and detecting crime. If successful, the new technology may lead to changes in policing strategies designed to enhance positive policing outcomes (e.g. improving police response time or reducing targeted crimes).

Section 9

Innovations in Justice Information Sharing

Overview

OJP, primarily through BJA and DOJ's Global Justice Information Sharing Initiative (Global), supports national policy, practices, and technology solutions to improve information sharing capacity within the criminal justice community, while emphasizing the importance of privacy and civil liberty protections and improving safety in our communities.

Each initiative described in this chapter requires a multidisciplinary response, executive sponsorship, stakeholder ownership, and collaborative program implementation to address operational, technical, and policy needs. The initiatives presented do not require a large investment of resources and will support DOJ's information sharing mission, improve the information sharing processes to strengthen decision making, and enable research and evaluation to identify promising practices with a strong return on investment.

In 2012, problem definition, coalition building, program design, training, and technical assistance will be critical to ensuring program processes are successful and replicable. In addition, field practitioners' insights will continue to be invaluable for developing targeted, sustainable solutions nationwide.

Discretionary Programs

Program Name National Information Exchange Model (NIEM) Program Support
FY 2012 Funding $900,000
OJP Sponsor BJA
Web Link www.niem.gov
Program Contact Chris Traver, (202) 307-2963, Christopher.Traver@usdoj.gov
Program Description
NIEM represents a vital partnership between the DOJ, DHS, and HHS, as well as the state, local, and tribal government agencies representative of each discipline. NIEM provides common tools and a data model to derive common standards by which to share information across jurisdictional boundaries more effectively. The competitively selected grantee will provide technical development and assistance to users to allow NIEM to continue to expand and mature across domains. In addition, these efforts will support domain self-service through the development of open tools and interface requirements, permitting individual NIEM partners to create their own customized tools and workflows. This flexibility means that NIEM will provide a higher level of service to its customers, while improving efficiency and reducing overall program costs.

Program Name Federated Identity, Privilege Management, and Technical Privacy Implementation
FY 2012 Funding $600,000
OJP Sponsor BJA
Web Link www.it.ojp.gov/gfipm
Program Contact Chris Traver, (202) 307-2963, Christopher.Traver@usdoj.gov
Program Description
Federated identity allows a single user to access multiple information systems with a single credential or login account. The participating systems agree to grant access to the user based on defined policies, as well as the specific attributes the user carries (e.g., training certification, intelligence analysis experience). This program is the Global Justice Information Sharing Initiative's (Global's) approach to bringing the federated identity concept to justice agencies and

jurisdictions. Using GFIPM, agencies can greatly expand the resources available to their users while providing adequate security and privacy controls and reducing overall costs.

This program will focus on delivery of Global-endorsed policy templates and guidelines to support GFIPM implementation in the field. It also will continue support of the National Information Exchange Federation (NIEF), a collaborative effort of Regional Information Sharing Systems, Homeland Security Information Network, Pennsylvania Justice Network, Criminal Information Sharing Alliance Network, and others. The NIEF delivery team is the initial user group for GFIPM, providing operational feedback and demonstrated results of the GFIPM program. This operational federation will continue to expand the services available to each member's user community, as well as to increase the number of participants.

Program Name SMART FY 12 Maintenance and Operation of the Dru Sjodin National Sex Offender Public Website
FY 2012 Funding $1,000,000
OJP Sponsor SMART Office
Web Link www.smart.gov or www.nsopw.gov/Core/Portal.aspx
Program Contact Samantha Opong, (202) 514-9320, Samantha.Opong@usdoj.gov
Program Description
The Dru Sjodin National Sex Offender Public Website (NSOPW) provides an opportunity for jurisdictions to participate in an unprecedented public safety resource by sharing public sex offender data nationwide, working collaboratively for the safety of both adults and children. First established in 2005, NSOPW was renamed by the Adam Walsh Child Protection and Safety Act of 2006 in honor of 22-year-old college student Dru Sjodin of Grand Forks, North Dakota, a young woman who was kidnapped and murdered by a sex offender who crossed state lines to commit his crime. NSOPW is the only government system that exists to link public state, territory, and tribal sex offender registries from one national search site. Parents, employers, and other concerned residents can utilize the Website's search tool as a safety resource to identify location information on sex offenders residing, working, and attending school not only in their own neighborhoods but in other nearby states and communities as well. In addition, the Website assists citizens with learning the facts about sexual abuse and how to protect themselves and loved ones from potential victimization.

Training and Technical Assistance

Program Name Justice Information Sharing Training and Technology Assistance
FY 2012 Funding $850,000
OJP Sponsor BJA
Web Link http://it.ojp.gov; www.niem.gov
Program Contact Chris Traver, (202) 307-2963, Christopher.Traver@usdoj.gov
Program Description
The project will continue the NIEM Practical Implementers Training Course and the online (eLearning) version of the course that can be completed on demand by users anywhere in the world. The recipient will support the National Information Sharing Standards (NISS) Helpdesk and Knowledgebase, a function that assists field practitioners through providing an online catalog of implementation questions and answers, as well as one-on-one email support for implementation questions. In addition, the grant recipient will be responsible for expanding the catalog of JIS related training services, to include at a minimum, the Global Reference Architecture and the GFIPM program.

Program Name Global Support For National Policy, Practice, and Technology
FY 2012 Funding $2,500,000
OJP Sponsor BJA
Web Link http://it.ojp.gov;
Program Contact Chris Traver, (202) 307-2963, Christopher.Traver@usdoj.gov
Program Description

The project will provide a TTA and implementation strategy that will meet the goals of the Program Manager for the Information Sharing Environment (PM-ISE) and DOJ's Global in Transforming the Justice and Public Safety Business Model. The applicant will be responsible for working closely with BJA to support DOJ's Global and related efforts, as well as coordinating with PM-ISE and all public and private stakeholders in order to inform project activities and evaluate outcomes.

Program Name Justice Information Sharing Architecture and Implementation Support
FY 2012 Funding $750,000
OJP Sponsor BJA
Web Link www.bja.gov
Program Contact David Lewis, (202) 616-7829, David.P.Lewis@usdoj.gov
Program Description
This program will provide training and technical assistance services on a variety of criminal justice topics related to information sharing. These could potentially include multiple projects to address specific training needs in areas such as data standards, service oriented architecture, federated identity, or privacy and security policy implementation. BJA seeks experienced national partner organizations with the demonstrated capacity to provide national scope services to assist justice practitioners in understanding and implementing information sharing capabilities utilizing a business-driven and architecture-based approach.

Program Name Improving Correctional Agency Information Sharing
FY 2012 Funding $600,000
OJP Sponsor BJA
Web Link www.bja.gov
Program Contact Chris Traver, (202) 307-2963, Christopher.Traver@usdoj.gov
Program Description
BJA is seeking applicants to support technical assistance (TA) and pilot site implementation to state, local, and tribal jurisdictions that result in justice information sharing enhancements which increase the effectiveness of offender management efforts. The applicant should propose and engage in collaborative partnership with appropriate organizations that have expertise in offender management strategies, in the translation of the contemporary justice research and literature into effective policies and practices, and in the implementation of strategies that leverage information sharing technology conforming with DOJ's Global standards and tools.

Program Name Crime Analysis Center Improvement Program
FY 2012 Funding $1,600,000
OJP Sponsor BJA
Web Link www.bja.gov
Program Contact Chris Traver, (202) 307-2963, Christopher.traver@usdoj.gov
Program Description
Crime Analysis Centers (CAC) represent an essential resource to criminal justice agencies, in particular to law enforcement. These CACs draw information from a wide variety of sources, both internal and external, to identify trends, correlate crimes, and propose solutions or mitigation strategies. However, not all agencies utilize the CAC concept to full effect, or even have a CAC capacity of any kind. The competitively selected grantee under this program will collaborate with CACs across the country to identify best practices, common challenges, and opportunities for advancement. The result will be a toolkit supporting evidence-based practices for replication nationwide.

Program Name State Criminal Justice Technology Coordination and Enhancements Program
FY 2012 Funding $300,000
OJP Sponsor BJA
Web Link www.bja.gov
Program Contact Chris Traver, (202) 307-2963, Christopher.traver@usdoj.gov
Program Description
Without strong leadership and coordination from a state level, criminal justice IT projects often

become fragmented, as local priorities and budget considerations outweigh state and national requirements for information sharing and interoperability. Advancements in technology can help maintain or improve operations in times of limited budgets, but adherence to national standards and best practices is essential to realize the full benefits of those advancements. This program will help ensure jurisdictions leverage evidence-based practices around data sharing, privacy protection, security, and interoperability at the state level, by engaging the SAA community and fostering state leadership and coordination of IT investments. This will not only improve how states, counties, and local jurisdictions implement information sharing, but also help BJA maximize the impact of grant funding by ensuring national policy is being adequately informed and disseminated.

Program deliverables will include training and technical assistance products that promote replication of information sharing best practices from an executive/policy level and targeted at state IT leaders; targeted communication methodologies; and pilot projects that demonstrate the value of supported solutions.

Program Name Federated Identity, Privilege Management, and Technical Privacy Implementation
FY 2012 Funding $800,000
OJP Sponsor BJA
Web Link http://www.it.ojp.gov
Program Contact Chris Traver, (202) 307-2963, Christopher.Traver@usdoj.gov
Program Description
This project will support the ISE and related initiatives in the full implementation of the Program Manager for the Information Sharing Environment (PM-ISE) Privacy Guidelines. The applicant will be responsible for supporting the ISE Privacy and Civil Liberties subcommittee of the Information Sharing and Access Interagency Policy Committee (ISA IPC) and updating the guidelines as required based on committee direction. The applicant will also implement a TTA program that will assist agencies and national programs on privacy, civil rights, and civil liberties (PCRCL) methods of adoption including Memoranda of Understanding (MOU), Privacy Act routine uses, and technology support/automation. The TTA program will enable adoption of appropriate PCRCL protections that are at least as comprehensive as the ISE Privacy Guidelines primarily among federal agencies, fusion centers, and private sector entities participating in the ISE.

Appendix A

Continuation Grants

Discretionary Programs

Program Name Identity Theft Victim Assistance Networks
Grantee Maryland Crime Victims' Resource Center, Inc.
FY 2012 Funding $250,000
OJP Sponsor OVC
Web Link www.ovc.gov
Program Contact Laura Ivkovich, (202) 616-3576, Laura.Ivkovich@usdoj.gov
Program Description
Through this program, OVC will unite the victim assistance field with new and existing victim service coalitions to assist victims of identity theft. OVC is funding the establishment of the infrastructure for a system of collaborative statewide and/or regional coalitions that will enable current victim advocates better to network, strengthen their collective victim assistance efforts, and foster improved communication with one another to improve the disparate response to the needs and rights of victims of identity theft nationwide.

OVC made one competitive award in FY 2010, with a supplemental award in FY 2011. With demonstrated success from previous years, OVC intends to make one final supplemental award to the current grantee to continue to develop the network of victim assistance programs serving identity theft victims, capable of addressing victims' unmet needs. OVC's program design calls for development over three years. The first year involved planning and outreach to current coalitions and victim programs about the impact of crime and the critical needs of this underserved population (2010). The second year involved the development of a solicitation and the competitive sub-awards to AZ, CO, ID, MN, NY, South Brooklyn, SC, TX, and WA—enabling these programs and coalitions to expand their reach of services to victims of identity theft and to share promising practices and models nationwide (2011). The third year will fund the continuation of training and technical assistance to the network of programs and coalitions, as well as an evaluation and replication of program efforts (2012).

Program Name American Indian and Alaska Nation Sexual Assault Nurse Examiner and Sexual Assault Response Team Program (AI/AN SANE-SART)
Grantee Mississippi Band of Choctaw Indians, Southern Indian Health Council, Inc., Tuba City Regional Health Care Corp.
FY 2012 Funding $225,000
OJP Sponsor OVC
Web Link www.ovc.gov
Program Contact Kathleen Gless, (202) 307-6049, Kathleen.Gless@usdoj.gov
Program Description
Through this program, OVC will continue to support the Mississippi Band of Choctaw Indians, Southern Indian Health Council, Inc., and Tuba City Regional Health Care Corp., projects to enhance their communities' capacity to provide high-quality, multidisciplinary, victim-centered services and support for adult and child victims of sexual assault. OVC made three competitive awards in FY 2011. With demonstrated success from the previous year, OVC intends to make a supplemental award to the current grantees to continue to develop the communities' capacity to enhance the response to victims of sexual assault. OVC's program design called for development over four years. The first year involved identifying a coordinator and the structure and members of the SART; conducting a comprehensive needs assessment; and developing a strategic plan (FY 2011). The second year of funding (FY 2012), the sites will focus on implementing the SANE-SART Program as determined by the Strategic Plan. Activities include launching the SANE-SART AI/AN project with the support of the SANE-SART TTA provider, OVC, and OVC's partners; assisting the sites in expanding their SANE-SARTs; developing protocols and policies; developing

or enhancing tribal codes; identifying training and technical assistance for SANE-SART; and identifying the means to acquire needed equipment.

Program Name Services for American Victims of Domestic Violence Overseas
Grantee Americans Overseas Domestic Violence Crisis Center
FY 2012 Funding $250,000
OJP Sponsor OVC
Web Link www.ovc.gov
Program Contact Sharron Chapman, (202) 305-2358, Sharron.Chapman@usdoj.gov
Program Description
This demonstration program supports one organization that will provide a range of services to American victims of domestic violence overseas, including but not limited to crisis hotline support, safety planning, counseling referrals, relocation assistance, and legal assistance. The grantee will be expected to support replication of the program through the development of a series of bulletins highlighting the project, to be published by OVC. The grantee will be required to work in close coordination with agencies funded under the Services for American Victims of Crime Overseas program, a broader initiative to address the needs of all American victims of overseas crimes other than domestic violence.

Program Name Victim Assistance and Compensation Professional Development Fellowship Program
Grantees Grace Call and Beverly Horn
FY 2012 Funding $274,519
OJP Sponsor OVC
Web Link www.ovc.gov
Program Contact Kisha Green, (202) 307-5983, kisha.w.green@usdoj.gov
Program Description
This program will award funding for continuation of up to two fellowships awarded in FY 2011 to assist OVC in its efforts to advance crime victims' rights and services. Fellows will support OVC by analyzing the existing data regarding services available for underserved crime victims; identifying trends and exploring ways to capture information about services for these victims; and analyzing the overall effectiveness of state Victims of Crime Act (VOCA) programs.

Program Name Victim Assistance Professional Development Fellowship Program
Grantees Bethany Case, Keely McCarthy, William Petty, and Debra Whitcomb
FY 2012 Funding $508,029
OJP Sponsor OVC
Web Link www.ovc.gov
Program Contact Sharron Chapman, (202) 305-2358, Sharron.Chapman@usdoj.gov
Program Description
This program will award funding for continuation of up to four fellowships to assist OVC in its efforts to advance crime victims' rights and services. Fellows will undertake special projects to provide direct operational assistance to crime victim organizations and agencies; design and develop innovative initiatives; implement a training strategy; and assist with evaluation and capacity building efforts, among other activities. Fellowships will specifically address underserved victims of crime and evidence-based training and technical assistance.

Program Name Post Secondary Education: Integrating Crime Victims' Issues into University and College Curricula
Grantee University of Massachusetts Lowell
FY 2012 Funding $200,000
OJP Sponsor OVC
Web Link www.ovc.gov
Program Contact Laura Ivkovich, (202) 616-3576, Laura.Ivkovich@usdoj.gov
Program Description
In FY 2009, OVC competitively funded the first round of a national demonstration program to integrate crime victims' issues into university and college curricula. Through this program, OVC

intends to provide comprehensive, quality education and training for future victim service providers and allied professionals. This strategic three-year initiative focuses on enhancing university and college curricula by integrating crime victimization issues and responses into multi-disciplinary education models and faculty development in universities and colleges. OVC made one competitive 18-month award to the grantee in 2009. Based upon successful demonstration of the grant activities, the second round of funding (2011) supported the development of curriculum kits, sample course modules, outreach materials, and evaluation. The third and final round of funding will finalize the course modules and outreach materials, complete an evaluation of these materials, and develop a replication guide.

Program Name National Field Generated Training, Technical Assistance and Demonstration Project
Grantee Various, see below
FY 2012 Funding $2,950,000
OJP Sponsor OVC
Web Link www.ovc.gov/ncvrw
Program Contacts Various, see below
Program Description
The National Field-Generated Training, Technical Assistance, and Demonstration Continuation Project (originally competed in FY 2011), supports 12 national-scope projects in seven topic areas to develop or enhance training, technical assistance, promising practices, models, and programs that build the capacity of victim services and ancillary providers. The overall objective of these projects is to enhance the provision of services and support to crime victims, and ensure they are afforded their rights. Topic areas include drunk and impaired driving; mortgage fraud; sexual assault within correctional settings; coordination of state-tribal victim services; long-term mental health and other consequences of mass violence; LGBTQ crime victims' access to mainstream victim services; and victim services for young male victims of crime.

1. **Grantee** Fund for the City of New York
   Program Contact Sharron Chapman (202) 305-2358, Sharron.Chapman@usdoj.gov
   Project Description The Center for Court Innovation will fund the Save Our Streets (SOS) Crown Heights Program as a demonstration project. This program will be enhanced by including in its case management services a victim service infrastructure that addresses young men of color and their families, who are victims of crime. The center will develop protocols for use between SOS and victim service agencies, implement culturally competent victim services and support groups, provide training on victimization for SOS staff, and create best practice documents and toolkits for violence intervention projects interested in replicating this effort.

2. **Grantee** Drexel University
   Program Contact Sharron Chapman (202) 305-2358, Sharron.Chapman@usdoj.gov
   Project Description The National Network of Hospital-Based Violence Intervention Programs (NNHVIP) at Drexel University is a network of more than 15 hospital-based intervention programs nationwide working with young male victims of color from hospital bedside through discharge. The project will provide training and technical assistance for NNHVIP frontline staff to enhance their ability to meet the needs of crime victims, specifically African-American and Latino males, by teaching NNHVIP staff to employ a trauma-informed approach to their work. This training and technical assistance approach will be developed and piloted for use by traditional victim service providers.

3. **Grantee** National Crime Prevention Council
   Program Contact Sharron Chapman (202) 305-2358, Sharron.Chapman@usdoj.gov
   Project Description The National Crime Prevention Council will implement the "Tips and Tools for Mortgage Fraud Victims Campaign," which will feature an online presence and tools for informing victims and educating victim service providers, attorneys, and state/local government officials about the many types of crimes associated with mortgage fraud and the best ways to serve its victims. The council also will conduct training for

victim service providers, both in person and through webinars, to improve their knowledge of mortgage fraud.

4. **Grantee** Just Detention International
   Program Contact Kimberly Kelberg (202) 305-2903, Kimberly.Kelberg@usdoj.gov
   Project Description Just Detention International (JDI) will partner with the Miami-Dade County Corrections and Rehabilitation Department (MDRC) and the Roxcy Bolton Rape Treatment Center to respond to victims of sexual violence occurring in the correctional setting of the Miami-Dade County, Florida, jail system. Sexual assault response teams, onsite confidential rape crisis counseling programs, and sexual assault inmate education programs will be developed within each MDRC facility. JDI will develop a resource guide for corrections officials and sexual abuse service providers nationwide to use in establishing programs in corrections and rehabilitation settings.

5. **Grantee** Vera Institute of Justice
   Program Contact Kimberly Kelberg (202) 305-2903, Kimberly.Kelberg@usdoj.gov
   Project Description The Vera Institute of Justice, through a partnership with the Johnson County Sheriffs, the Johnson County Department of Corrections (DOC), and the Metropolitan Organization to Counter Sexual Assault, will connect adult and juvenile victims of corrections-based sexual violence, who are housed in the local jail, the residential work release program, or the juvenile detention center with community-based sexual assault victim service providers. Vera also will design and implement a facility-based Sexual Assault Response Team within the adult work release and juvenile detention programs of the DOC. Deliverables include a toolkit for jails, community confinement facilities, and juvenile detention centers on how to work with community-based sexual assault victim advocates.

6. **Grantee** Mothers Against Drunk Driving
   Program Contact Jasmine D'Addario-Fobian (202) 305-3332, Jasmine.D'Addario-Fobian@usdoj.gov
   Project Description Mothers Against Drunk Driving (MADD) will develop and facilitate a specialized training institute to increase competent service delivery to underserved victim groups nationwide. MADD will implement a 20-hour training institute for each year of the project to enhance the knowledge base of the unique needs and issues of these populations, develop and implement a volunteer management component with the training institute, and develop strategic community outreach plans specific to the unique needs of each population.

7. **Grantee** National Indian Justice Center
   Program Contact Jasmine D'Addario-Fobian (202) 305-3332, Jasmine.D'Addario-Fobian@usdoj.gov
   Project Description The National Indian Justice Center will work to improve tribal and non-Indian justice system responses to American Indian and Alaska Native victims of alcohol-related crashes on and near tribal lands by developing a model "one-stop shop" training and technical assistance program for victim service providers. The program will be pilot tested with 10 or more tribal and non-Indian justice systems nationally and disseminated to six other Tribal Transportation TTA Programs.

8. **Grantee** New York City Gay and Lesbian Anti-Violence Project
   Program Contact Jasmine D'Addario-Fobian (202) 305-3332, Jasmine.D'Addario-Fobian@usdoj.gov
   Project Description In partnership with the National Center for Victims of Crime and the Vera Institute of Justice, the New York City Gay and Lesbian Anti-Violence Project will implement a national demonstration project to create, test, and evaluate victim service models and policies, correlated with the necessary TTA, and to replicate strategies that will provide equal access to mainstream victim services for LGBTQ survivors. The project will determine primary indicators for success; establish a national advisory committee for

feedback and review of all project stages; implement baseline and annual evaluations; develop and implement strategies for addressing gaps in services, and barriers to accessing these services in mainstream organizations; create a compendium of strategies and materials for national TTA; and develop protocols for outreach, advocacy, and services that will increase LGBTQ competency throughout mainstream victim services through a national dissemination plan.

9. **Grantee** Beyond Diversity Resource Center
   Program Contact Jasmine D'Addario-Fobian (202) 305-3332, Jasmine.D'Addario-Fobian@usdoj.gov
   Project Description The Beyond Diversity Resource Center, in partnership with the School of Social Work–Rutgers, the State University of New Jersey, will implement a demonstration project with six mainstream victim service providers from across the United States. The center will implement organizational development strategies with the participating organizations, offer relevant diversity training, and develop organizational protocols in an effort to enhance LGBTQ victim services. A compendium of project research, organizational development interventions, and provider best practices will be developed for use by OVC.

10. **Grantee** King County Coalition Against Domestic Violence
    Program Contact Jasmine D'Addario-Fobian (202) 305-3332, Jasmine.D'Addario-Fobian@usdoj.gov
    Project Description King County Coalition Against Domestic Violence (KCCADV), in partnership with the North West Network of Bisexual, Trans, Lesbian & Gay Survivors of Abuse (NW Network), will create a nationally replicable model for improving lesbian, bisexual, transgender, transsexual, gay, and queer crime victims' access to mainstream services. The proposal includes a regional response model, which will mobilize mainstream victim service programs throughout King County, Washington, to work together to ensure broad and meaningful access to LGBTQ victims. The project will support 15–30 improvement sites, which will adopt specific access recommendations; create regional response workgroups to develop practice and policy recommendations; advance policy advocacy through established crime-victim coalitions; and compile a regional response national replication toolkit.

11. **Grantee** Oklahoma District Attorney's Council
    Program Contact Joel Hall (202) 307-3940, Joel.Hall@usdoj.gov
    Project Description The State-Tribal Crime Victim Liaison Demonstration Program will develop meaningful communication and coordination between the grantee and the surrounding tribal communities. This program is intended to greatly improve communication among federal, state, local, and tribal officials; foster more collaborative partnerships; and enhance victim assistance and outreach services to and among tribal communities from state-administered programs, allied agencies, and organizations. The project will include an in-state crime victim liaison with extensive knowledge of and respect for tribal values, cultures, and traditions, as well as practical victim services experience and an exceptional knowledge of tribal and public crime victim assistance and compensation programs.

12. **Grantee** Voices of September 11, Inc.
    Program Contact Barbara Robertson (202) 353-3775, Barbara.Robertson2@usdoj.gov
    Project Description Voices of September 11 will provide communities with a resource kit to guide organizations through creating an infrastructure that effectively responds to the immediate needs of victims affected by mass violence, as well as an understanding of the support model necessary to address long-term needs. Phase I of the project will define key information needed for a resource kit; phase II will develop, test, and evaluate the kit; and in phase III, OVC will work closely with the grantee to institute an effective national rollout of the kit.

Program Name SMART FY12 Maintenance and Operation of Dru Sjodin National Sex Offender Public Website
Grantee Institute for Intergovernmental Research
FY 2012 Funding TBD
OJP Sponsor SMART Office
Web Link www.smart.gov or http://www.nsopw.gov/Core/Portal.aspx
Program Contact Samantha Opong, (202) 514-9320, Samantha.Opong@usdoj.gov
Program Description
The Dru Sjodin National Sex Offender Public Website (NSOPW) provides an opportunity for jurisdictions to participate in an unprecedented public safety resource by sharing public sex offender data nationwide, working collaboratively for the safety of both adults and children. First established in 2005, NSOPW was renamed by the Adam Walsh Child Protection and Safety Act of 2006 in honor of 22-year-old college student Dru Sjodin of Grand Forks, North Dakota, a young woman who was kidnapped and murdered by a sex offender who crossed state lines to commit his crime. NSOPW is the only government system that exists to link public state, territory, and tribal sex offender registries on one national search site. Parents, employers, and other concerned residents can utilize the Website's search tool as a safety resource to identify location information on sex offenders residing, working, and attending school not only in their own neighborhoods but also in other nearby states and communities. The Website also will help citizens learn the facts about sexual abuse and ways to protect themselves and loved ones from potential victimization.

Program Name CIO & State Coordination for Information Sharing and Technology Coordination
Grantee National Association of State Chief Information Officers (NASCIO)
FY 2012 Funding $200,000
OJP Sponsor BJA
Web Link www.nascio.org/committees/ea
Program Contact Chris Traver, (202) 307-2963, Christopher.Traver@usdoj.gov
Program Description
This program is designed to encourage coordination among state leaders with regard to national standards and best practices in enterprise architecture and governance. By fostering more active relationships, DOJ, the Global Justice Information Sharing Initiative, and state Chief Information Officers (CIOs) and their staff can adopt and coordinate information sharing across all levels of government. State CIOs are responsible for many areas of government, and emphasis on justice-specific challenges and planning efforts is increasingly critical to the effectiveness of national programs supported by BJA and stakeholders in the field.

Training and Technical Assistance

Program Name State Victim Assistance Academy (SVAA) Continuation
FY 2012 Funding $400,000
Grantees: Indiana Coalition Against Sexual Assault/IN, Justice and Public Safety Cabinet/KY, Creighton University/NE, and Fox Valley Technical College/WI
OJP Sponsor OVC
Web Link www.ovc.gov
Program Contact Richard Greenough, (202) 616-8715, Richard.greenough2@usdoj.gov
Program Description
This program will provide continuation funding up to $100,000 each to continue support for State Victim Assistance Academies (SVAAs) in four states (Indiana, Kentucky, Nebraska and Wisconsin). SVAAs provide training to develop skills of victim assistance providers from community- and systems-based programs. For more information on where OVC-funded SVAAs are located, visit www.ovc.gov/assist/existingsvaa.html.

Program Name Harold Rogers Prescription Drug Monitoring Training and Technical Assistance Program
Grantee Brandeis University
FY 2012 Funding $1,200,000

OJP Sponsor BJA
Web Link www.bja.gov/funding.aspx
Program Contact Danica Szarvas-Kidd, (202) 305-7418, Danica.Szarvas-Kidd@usdoj.gov
Program Description
BJA partners with Brandeis University to provide training and technical assistance to grantees and states that are planning for a PDMP. The assistance will include online, telephone, and onsite assistance to states seeking to build or enhance PDMPs; facilitation of regular communication among PDMP peers in the field; the identification and facilitation of training opportunities for grantees; national and regional meetings; reporting of PDMP trends; and assisting grantees in collecting and reporting on the program performance measures.

In addition, BJA will seek to enhance the National PDMP Clearinghouse/Center of Excellence that will serve as a clearinghouse of information, research findings, evaluation results and tools, statistics, epidemiological examinations, and other materials relevant to PDMP administrators, state and federal policy makers, and researchers. The center will develop methods and vehicles for states to report on PDMP operations and effectiveness and undertake projects that highlight best practices for PDMPs.

Program Name VALOR
Institute for Intergovernmental Research
FY 2012 Funding $1,786,883
OJP Sponsor BJA
Web Link www.bja.gov/funding.aspx
Program Contact Deborah Meader, (202) 305-2601, Deborah.Meader@usdoj.gov
Program Description
Funds will support a national officer safety training and technical assistance (TTA) program that will continue to support a wide range of multi-level training; promote a culture of safety within agencies and personnel; and, ultimately, save officers' lives. Funding may be divided between a non-competitive supplemental award and a competitive solicitation to continue providing TTA on officer safety issues, as well as expand the focus of VALOR and officer safety.

Program Name National Gang Center
Grantee Institute for Intergovernmental Research
FY 2012 Funding $1,500,000
OJP Sponsor OJJDP
Web Link www.ojjdp.gov
Program Contact Dennis Mondoro, (202)514-3913, Dennis.Mondoro@ usdoj.gov
Program Description
OJJDP will continue to fund, in partnership with BJA, a National Gang Center to provide TTA to law enforcement agencies and communities on gang prevention and intervention programs and strategies. The National Gang Center also will administer the annual National Youth Gang Survey and disseminate current research and practice on gang prevention, intervention, and suppression strategies and programs.

Program Name Children's Advocacy Centers
Grantee National Children's Alliance
FY 2012 Funding $15,700,000
OJP Sponsor OJJDP
Web Link www.nationalchildrensalliance.org/
Program Contact Lou Ann Holland, (202) 305-2742, Lou.Ann.Holland@usdoj.gov
Program Description
OJJDP will provide continuation funding to programs that improve the coordinated investigation and prosecution of child abuse cases. These programs include funding for a national subgrant program for local children's advocacy centers; a membership and accreditation program; regional children's advocacy centers; and specialized technical assistance and training programs for child abuse professionals and prosecutors. Local children's advocacy centers bring together

multidisciplinary teams of professionals to coordinate the investigation, treatment, and prosecution of child abuse cases.

Program Name Court Appointed Special Advocate Programs
Grantee National CASA Association
FY 2012 Funding $3,900,000
OJP Sponsor OJJDP
Web Link www.nationalcasa.org
Program Contact Cecilia Duquela, (202) 514-9372, Cecilia.Duquela@usdoj.gov
Program Description
OJJDP will provide continuation funding to support Court Appointed Special Advocates (CASA) programs across the country. CASA programs provide children in the foster care system or at risk of entering the dependency system with high-quality, timely, effective, and sensitive representation before the court. CASA programs train and support volunteers who advocate for the best interests of the child in dependency proceedings. OJJDP funds a national CASA TTA provider and a national membership and accreditation organization to support state and local CASA organizations' efforts to recruit volunteer advocates, including minority volunteers, and to provide TTA to these organizations and to stakeholders in the child welfare system.

Program Name Seventh National SART Training Conference
Grantee Minneapolis Medical Research Foundation (SANE-SART Resource Service)
FY 2012 Funding $0 (Funding was provided in FY 2011)
OJP Sponsor OVC
Web Link www.sane-sart.com
Program Contact Olivia Schramm, (202) 616-8803, Olivia.Schramm@usdoj.gov
Program Description
The 2013 Seventh National Sexual Assault Response Team (SART) Training Conference will provide three days of state-of-the-art training for SART professionals, including victim advocates, sexual assault nurse examiners (SANEs) and other medical personnel, crime lab specialists, prosecutors, and law enforcement. The conference also will offer specialized training to address issues specific to sexual assault in Indian Country. National experts in the five SART disciplines and experts from Indian Country will present conference workshops and keynotes on a multidisciplinary, victim-centered approach to sexual assault, to improve the care provided to sexual assault victims. The conference offers SART scholarships, law enforcement scholarships, and tribal team scholarships. This conference has been held every two years since 2001, and continuation funding will be used for the planning and implementation of the 2013 SART Conference. The project period is 24 months, and the 2009 award was supplemented in FY 2011.

Program Name American Indian and Alaska Native Sexual Assault Nurse Examiner and Sexual Assault Response Team Program (AI/AN SANE-SART)
Grantee Tribal Law and Policy Institute (TLPI)
FY 2012 Funding $100,000
OJP Sponsor OVC
Web Link www.ovc.gov
Program Contact Kathleen Gless, (202) 307-6049, Kathleen.Gless@usdoj.gov
Program Description
Through this program, OVC will continue to support the Tribal Law and Policy Institute (TLPI), which demonstrates recognition of, and experience with the importance of culture, history, traditions, and spirituality inherent in the AI/AN community, as well as the value of adapting community and evidence-based sexual assault intervention strategies for tribal communities. In the first year of the program (FY 2011), TLPI focused on supporting the AI/AN SANE-SART sites in conducting comprehensive community needs assessments and developing strategic plans to enhance and build sustainable, culturally relevant, victim-centered SANE-SART projects. The second year of funding (FY 2012) will have a much greater focus on the development and implementation of TTA, and coordination and communication with OVC and its partners. Potential activities include assisting the sites in launching their strategic SANE-SART AI/AN

project; creating new or modifying existing sexual assault protocols and policies that enhance response to sexual assault; developing or enhancing tribal codes; and identifying TTA for OVC's project staff and partners, SARTs, SANEs, and community stakeholders.

Program Name 2013 National Crime Victims' Rights Week (NCVRW) Community Awareness Project
Grantee National Association of VOCA Assistance Administrators
FY 2012 Funding $375,000
OJP Sponsor OVC
Web Link www.ovc.gov
Program Contact Olivia Schramm, (202) 616-8803, Olivia.Schramm@usdoj.gov
Program Description
This cooperative agreement supports the provision of financial and technical assistance to 60 communities nationwide to conduct public education and awareness activities on crime victims' rights and services in their jurisdictions during the 2013 National Crime Victims' Rights Week (NCVRW). The objectives and deliverables for this cooperative agreement are to promote 2013 NCVRW events, victims' rights and services; develop and administer the community project outreach and application process; establish a review committee to review, grade, and comment on each application; advertise and publicize the funding availability through OVC and other public venues; establish an NCVRW Community Awareness Project Web site to advertise the funding opportunity; and provide technical assistance to each selected subrecipient organization through use of an interactive Internet-based video conferencing program and individual consultation via e-mail and telephone. This funding would continue support for one cooperative agreement for an additional 12 months

Program Name 2013 National Crime Victims' Rights Week (NCVRW) Resource Guide
Grantee National Center for Victims of Crime
FY 2012 Funding $350,000
OJP Sponsor OVC
Web Link www.ovc.gov/ncvrw
Program Contact Kimberly Kelberg, (202) 305-2903, Kimberly.Kelberg@usdoj.gov
Program Description
Since 1986, the NCVRW Resource Guide has assisted local victims, survivors, advocates, and communities in planning and preparing for their own annual commemoration of NCVRW. Through this cooperative agreement, OVC will continue its efforts to produce this valuable resource guide for the field to serve as the impetus for communities to generate greater awareness among crime victims, survivors, and allied professionals about victims' rights and services. In FY 2012, OVC will fund the National Center for Victims of Crime to develop the 2013 NCVRW Resource Guide, a customizable resource guide containing materials such as posters, model speeches, press releases, public service announcements, camera-ready artwork, and crime victimization statistical overviews for use by the field when planning local NCVRW events. The comprehensive kit will serve as a resource for communities to support efforts to heighten the public's awareness of crime victim issues nationwide during NCVRW in April 2013 and throughout the year.

Program Name U.S. Postal Inspection Service (USPIS) Public Awareness Campaign in Support of National Crime Victims' Rights Week
Grantee USPIS
FY 2012 Funding $255,000
OJP Sponsor OVC
Web Link www.ovc.gov
Program Contact Charlotte Clarke, (202) 514-2545, Charlotte.Clarke@usdoj.gov
Program Description
Crime Victims Fund discretionary resources support OVC's collaborative partnership with USPIS to target post office customers around the nation in April to help raise awareness of victims' rights and available services. Posters highlighting National Crime Victims' Rights Week will be displayed in more than 15,000 post offices serving more than 8 million customers per week.

Additionally, counter displays containing take-away cards highlighting how to "Get Help or Help Out" and listing toll free numbers for national victim assistance organizations will be made available. The cards also will be mailed to customers using the Postal Service's stamp delivery service.

Program Name Drug Market Intervention Initiative
Grantee Michigan State University
FY 2011 Funding $200,000
OJP Sponsor BJA
Web Link www.bja.gov/Publications/DMII.pdf
Program Contact James Chavis, (202) 307-0688, James.Chavis@usdoj.gov
Program Description
In 2007, through Project Safe Neighborhoods (PSN), BJA created a training and technical assistance project for local teams interested in implementing an open-air drug market intervention (DMI) initiative that is commonly referred to as the High Point model. DMI addresses the challenge of effectively responding to illegal drug markets, and their associated crime, violence, and disorder, that has proved challenging for communities and law enforcement for decades. DMI is a strategic problem-solving initiative to permanently eliminate open-air drug markets. The strategy targets individual geographic drug markets and prosecutes the most violent offenders as examples. The strategy then targets low level offenders and stages an intervention with families and community leaders. Law enforcement mobilizes community residents, leaders, and family members of low level drug dealers to voice their intolerance for this criminal behavior and to create opportunities and support for the offenders. Offenders are given the opportunity to correct criminal behavior (or face lengthy prison sentences) and are provided assistance in locating employment, housing, transportation, health care, and access to other social services. This initiative consists of three trainings for up to 10 target sites interested in replicating the strategy. Each selected site's team consists of a law enforcement officer, local prosecutor, community leader, and social service provider who attend all three trainings. Each team receives a site visit from a BJA technical assistance provider along with ongoing support to help local teams adapt the model to their unique local context.

Program Name Judicial Training
Grantee National Judicial College (NJC)
FY 2011 Funding $500,000
OJP Sponsor BJA
Web Link www.judges.org
Program Contact Kim Ball, (202) 307-2076, Kim.Ball@usdoj.gov
Program Description
BJA partners with NJC to provide judges the opportunity to enhance their judicial skills through courses and programs designed specifically to meet the needs of our changing judiciary. BJA and NJC work with chief justices, state court administrators, and state judicial educators to ensure that judges have scholarship opportunities to participate in these educational experiences. The courses offered range from the two-week "General Jurisdiction" course for new judges, to courses for experienced judges, such as "Advanced Evidence and Decision Making," and from specialized training, such as "Practical Approaches to Substance Abuse Issues and Co-occurring Mental and Substance Abuse Disorders," to skills-based courses such as "Judicial Writing and Enhancing Judicial Bench Skills."

Program Name Reducing Electronic Crime
Grantee National White Collar Crime Center (NW3C)
FY 2012 Funding $6,291,891
OJP Sponsor BJA
Web Link www.bja.gov
Program Contact David Lewis, (202) 616-7829, David.P.Lewis@usdoj.gov
Program Description
This program will improve the capacity of local criminal justice systems and provide national support for training and technical assistance that strategically addresses electronic and cyber

crime needs. The FY 2012 program will focus on funding national training and technical assistance efforts to:

- provide training curricula specializing in high tech crime, including but not limited to intelligence, cyber, and computer forensics, through innovative delivery methodologies such as training, roll call training, and academy training of both new recruits and experienced officers, prosecutors, and other justice system employees;
- provide train-the-trainer classes to expand the ability of more individuals to attend these types of classes without the cost of extensive travel;
- provide support to fusion centers and analysts in the areas of training and support materials;
- provide technical assistance to public safety agencies in the areas of investigation, training, intelligence, and computer forensics; and
- identify new crime trends in the area of high tech crime and develop methods for addressing these trends in the areas of training, education, and use of technology.

Program Name State Legislative Education and Action Project
Grantee National Conference of State Legislatures (NCSL)
FY 2012 Funding $75,000
OJP Sponsor BJA
Web Link www.bja.gov
Program Contact Lesley Buchan, (202) 305-0517, Lesley.Buchan@usdoj.gov
Program Description
NCSL, in a cooperative partnership with BJA, works to educate and inform state legislators and legislative staff in the 50 states and territories on priority criminal justice issues. The project fosters leadership capacity in state legislatures for examining cost-effective public safety and corrections options; and facilitates communication among state leaders on issues related to evidence-based planning and policies, reentry and recidivism reduction. Project objectives involve convening meetings and preparing publications on topics that explore and illustrate data-driven criminal justice approaches. The project employs the infrastructure of NCSL forums and products that are recognizable and credible to state lawmakers and their staff, to provide information that helps guide decision making.

Program Name Technical Assistance and Justice Policy Program
Grantee SEARCH Group, Inc.
FY 2012 Funding TBD
OJP Sponsor BJS
Web Link bjs.ojp.usdoj.gov
Program Contact Devon B. Adams, (202) 514-9157, Devon.Adams@usdoj.gov
Project Description
This project provides technical assistance and justice information policy assistance to states under the National Criminal History Improvement Program (NCHIP) and the NICS Improvement Amendments Act to enhance and improve criminal history record systems. Technical assistance will include direct onsite visits, telephone services, national and regional conferences and workshops, training sessions, and data collection and publication of criminal history related surveys and materials. Technical assistance provided will enable state participation in the National Crime Prevention and Privacy Compact and the National Fingerprint File.

Research and Statistical Programs

Program Name National Juvenile Probation Census Project
Grantee Westat, Inc.
FY 2012 Funding $400,000
OJP Sponsor OJJDP
Web Link www.ojjdp.gov
Program Contact Brecht Donoghue, (202) 305-1270, Brecht.Donoghue@usdoj.gov

Program Description
OJJDP will provide continuation funding to support the next round of its Census of Juveniles on Probation, which describes youth under justice supervision and the services they receive. The census provides critical data on the characteristics of youth on probation, the nature of their offenses, and how they are served. The number of youth on probation is roughly five times that of the population of youth in custody.

Program Name Justice Reinvestment
Grantees Council of State Governments Justice Center, Vera Institute of Justice, Center for Effective Public Policy, Criminal and Justice Institute
FY 2012 Funding $5,360,649
OJP Sponsor BJA
Web Link www.bja.gov/ProgramDetails.aspx?Program_ID=92
Program Contact Gary Dennis, (202) 305-9059, Gary.Dennis@usdoj.gov; Thurston Bryant, (202) 514-8082, Thurston.Bryant@usdoj.gov
Program Description
Justice Reinvestment is a data-driven approach designed to reduce corrections spending and redirect savings to alternative criminal justice strategies aimed at increasing public safety. Based on the collection and analyses of corrections, court, crime, and resource data, the drivers of state and local criminal justice system costs are identified. Policy responses and evidence-based practices are then developed to support a strategic plan to reduce costs and invest the resulting savings in services, programs, and activities designed to prevent crime and shore up the communities that are hardest hit by the incarceration and return of criminal justice populations. The ultimate goal is to achieve greater public safety at a lower cost while supporting more prevention-oriented and community-focused strategies.

Program Name Deaths in Custody Reporting Program, 2012-2015 Data Collection
Grantee Research Triangle Institute (RTI)
FY 2012 Funding $1,400,000
OJP Sponsor BJS
Web Link bjs.ojp.usdoj.gov
Program Contact William Sabol, (202) 514-1062, William.Sabol@usdoj.gov
Program Description
This program involves the collection of data from 50 state prisons and approximately 3,000 local jails on each death occurring in custody during the four calendar years from 2012 through 2015. Historically, there have been about 4,000 such deaths annually. The data will be collected using a Web-based data collection tool. Each annual collection cycle will start on January 1 and run for approximately 15 to 18 months to allow time for state Departments of Correction (DOC) and local jail administrators to obtain information about the final determinations of causes of death from medical examiners or other officials that certify causes of death occurring late in a calendar year. A separate, annual summary collection that requests information on the total number of deaths occurring within each DOC and local jail will be fielded near the end of each calendar year, and the individual death records will be reconciled to the summary count of death records. Complete and final data files for each calendar year will be available by the middle of the following calendar year. A one-time special collection of data on jail facility management as it relates to prevention of jail deaths also will be included within the project.

Program Name Annual Survey of Probation and Parole, 2011-2014
Grantee Westat, Inc.
FY 2012 Funding $280,000
OJP Sponsor BJS
Web Link bjs.ojp.usdoj.gov
Program Contact William Sabol, (202) 514-1062, William.Sabol@usdoj.gov
Program Description
Annually since 1977, BJS has collected yearend counts and yearly movements of community corrections populations through its Annual Parole Survey and Annual Probation Surveys. This program implements data collection activities associated with BJS's annual surveys of probation

and parole agencies. The two establishment surveys involve contact with 55 parole respondents for data on parole populations, and 467 probation respondents, consisting of some state and many local agencies. Data from these surveys provide the only comprehensive overview of the total community supervision population, as well as the parole and probation populations at both the national and state levels. The data gathered in the surveys provide the only national data of (1) "point-in-time" estimates of the prevalence of community supervision in the United States; (2) state-level estimates of these populations; (3) movements of offenders entering, by type of entry, and exiting, by type of exit, community supervision: (4) the characteristics of these offenders: and (5) outcomes of these offenders, including the number who had their sentence revoked and the reincarceration rate of parolees (i.e., recidivism measures).

Program Name Survey of Prison Inmates, 2012
Grantee Research Triangle Institute (RTI)
FY 2012 Funding $3,500,000
OJP Sponsor BJS
Web Link bjs.ojp.usdoj.gov
Program Contact William Sabol, (202) 514-1062, William.Sabol@usdoj.gov
Program Description
This program implements the Survey of Prison Inmates (SPI) which will collect data from up to 20,000 state and federal prison inmates in approximately 350 facilities to provide for national-level estimates of prison and jail inmate populations, as well as jurisdiction-level estimates for prisons holding more than 50,000 inmates (Bureau of Prisons (BOP), CA, TX, FL, and NY). The SPI will consist of a survey of a cross-sectional sample of state and federal prison inmates that can be used to produce nationally-representative estimates of harm, risk, and need in these populations, and that can produce jurisdiction-level estimates for the five largest prison systems (BOP, CA, TX, FL, and NY). Interviews are expected to last between 45 minutes and one hour and consist of a combination of CAPI and ACASI modes of administration, with CAPI being used to obtain background information and concepts that pose measurement challenges and ACASI being used for questions of a more sensitive nature. The goals of SIPLJ are to provide information about incarcerated populations and the harm they impose on society; their risk of recidivism; their programming needs; and the prevalence of these needs in reentry populations.

Program Name Annual Survey of Jails
Grantee: U.S. Census Bureau
FY 2012 Funding TBD
OJP Sponsor BJS
Web Link bjs.ojp.usdoj.gov
Program Contact William Sabol, (202) 514-1062, William.Sabol@usdoj.gov
Program Description:
This survey annually collects data from a nationally-representative sample of local jails and annually reports estimates of the size, composition, and change in jail populations nationwide. Key statistics reported include the number of jail inmates; the average daily population; rated capacity; capacity utilization (crowding); admissions into and releases from jails; and sex and race of jail inmates. Published statistics also describe changes in these characteristics. The Annual Survey of Jails series is a continuously-running, annual collection that BJS began in 1982.

Program Name National Prisoner Statistics (NPS-1)
Grantee U.S. Census Bureau
FY 2012 Funding TBD
OJP Sponsor BJS
Web Link bjs.ojp.usdoj.gov
Program Contact William Sabol, (202) 514-1062, William.Sabol@usdoj.gov
Program Description
National Prisoners Statistics is the longest running series in BJS' corrections collections. Begun in 1926 by an act of Congress, the NPS has annually measured the size of and change in state and federal prison populations. Key statistics reported from the program include the number of

prisoners, prison admissions and releases, incarceration rate, and demographic and offense distributions of prisoners.

Program Name National Corrections Reporting Program (NCRP)
Grantee Abt Associates
FY 2012 Funding $800,000
OJP Sponsor BJS
Web Link bjs.ojp.usdoj.gov
Program Contact William Sabol, (202) 514-1062, William.Sabol@usdoj.gov
Program Description
The NCRP collects administrative records about inmates admitted into and released from state prisons, in state prisons at yearend, and discharged from parole. Records contain information about types and date of admission; offenses and sentences; types and date of release; and method and dates of discharge from parole. Records also report offenses and sentences for up to three offenses, age, race, sex of inmates, and other measures of the incarceration experience. The NCRP data have been collected annually since 1983 with the exception of the inmate yearend custody data, which have been collected annually since 1999.

Program Name Capital Punishment, 2010-2012
Grantee U.S. Census Bureau
FY 2012 Funding TBD
OJP Sponsor BJS
Web Link bjs.ojp.usdoj.gov
Program Contact William Sabol, (202) 514-1062, William.Sabol@usdoj.gov
Program Description
Ensuring fairness in the administration of death sentences is of overriding importance. The annual collection of information by BJS on the laws authorizing the death penalty and characteristics and dispositions of persons who have been sentenced to death is critical to describing the administration of justice in this country and the use of its most severe sanctions. Since 1973, the collection and analysis of these data has been carried out by BJS, with the Census Bureau acting as the collecting agent. The National Prisoner Statistics (NPS) Program-8 fits within the larger BJS portfolio of surveys that inform the nation on the nature and composition inmates sentenced to state and federal prisons. The NPS-8 allows BJS to examine not only the small subset of inmates who have been sentenced to death, but also to track changes in the laws that guide who may receive these most punitive sentences.

Program Name National Crime Victimization Survey
Grantee U.S. Census Bureau
FY 2012 Funding $33,000,000
OJP Sponsor BJS
Web Link bjs.ojp.usdoj.gov
Program Contact William Sabol, (202) 514-1062, William.Sabol@usdoj.gov
Program Description
This program provides support for the continued development, collection, and processing of the National Crime Victimization Survey (NCVS). Each year, data are obtained from a nationally representative sample of households and persons on the frequency, characteristics, and consequences of criminal victimization in the United States. The NCVS collects information on violent and property victimization, both reported and not reported to police. The survey enables BJS to estimate the likelihood of victimization by rape, sexual assault, robbery, assault, theft, household burglary, and motor vehicle theft for the population as a whole, as well as for segments of the population such as women, the elderly, members of various racial groups, city dwellers, or other groups. The survey is administered by the U.S. Census Bureau (under the U.S. Department of Commerce) on behalf of BJS. The core program supports tasks related to sampling, instrument design, data collection, and processing.

Program Name Assessment and Collection of Administrative Data on Elder Abuse, Mistreatment, and Neglect
Grantee The Urban Institute
FY 2012 Funding $150,000
OJP Sponsor BJS
Web Link bjs.ojp.usdoj.gov
Program Contact Howard Snyder, (202) 616-8305, Howard.Snyder@usdoj.gov
Program Description
This program seeks proposals to examine the problem of elder abuse, mistreatment, and neglect through the collection of data on cases of suspected elder abuse referred to Adult Protective Services (APS) agencies, and cases reported to local law enforcement and prosecutors. The goals of this program are (1) to examine the characteristics of cases of suspected elder abuse referred to APS and/or reported to police in order to understand routes of reporting of elder abuse, as well as whether certain case characteristics impact case outcomes; and (2) to ascertain the feasibility of an ongoing and expanded collection of administrative data on cases of suspected elder abuse, mistreatment, and neglect.

Program Name Firearm Inquiry Statistics Program
Grantee Regional Justice Information Services (REJIS)
FY 2012 Funding $500,000
OJP Sponsor BJS
Web Link bjs.ojp.usdoj.gov
Program Contact Devon B. Adams, (202) 514-9157, Devon.Adams@usdoj.gov
Program Description
BJS initiated the program in 1995 to provide national estimates of the total number of firearm purchase applications received and denied pursuant to the Brady Act and similar state laws. The FIST program collects counts of firearm transfers and permit checks conducted by state and local agencies and combines this information with the FBI's National Instant Criminal Background Check System (NICS) transaction data. Additional information is collected on reasons for denials, appeals of denials, and law enforcement actions taken by the FBI and the Bureau of Alcohol, Tobacco, Firearms, and Explosives (ATF) against denied persons.

Program Name Arrest-Related Deaths Program, 2011-2014
Grantee Research Triangle Institute (RTI)
FY 2012 Funding TBD
OJP Sponsor BJS
Web Link bjs.ojp.usdoj.gov
Program Contact Joel Garner, (202) 305-2682, Joel.Garner@usdoj.gov
Program Description
This program implements the BJS Arrest Related Death (ARD) data collection program and the testing of alternative mechanisms to identify eligible cases and to collect accurate, timely and relevant information about these deaths. The program currently uses state-level reporting agents to identify arrest-related deaths and to obtain information about (1) the characteristics of the deceased, (2) the manner and cause of death, and (3) the interaction between the deceased and the law enforcement officer(s) involved.

Program Name 2011 National Survey of Indigent Defense Services
Grantee National Opinion Research Center (NORC)
FY 2012 Funding $415,000
OJP Sponsor BJS
Web Link bjs.ojp.usdoj.gov
Program Contact Howard Snyder, (202) 616-8305, Howard.Snyder@usdoj.gov
Program Description
This program is designing and implementing a national survey capable of describing the scope and operations of all indigent defense systems in the US. The project will involve a census of all jurisdictions to determine the type of indigent defense system operating in that jurisdiction. The

census, which will be informed by previous BJS data collections and input from various professional organizations, will collect basic information about the delivery of indigent defense services, including the type of indigent defense used, how indigent defense counsel is assigned, who is responsible for assigning indigent defense counsel, and what organization is responsible for tracking the costs and performance measures related to the delivery of indigent defense.

Program Name Census of Tribal Courts
Grantee Kauffman & Associates
FY 2012 Funding $200,000
OJP Sponsor BJS
Web Link bjs.ojp.usdoj.gov
Program Contact Howard Snyder, (202) 616-8305, Howard.Snyder@usdoj.gov
Program Description
This program seeks proposals for the collection of administrative and operational information on the tribal courts operating in the estimated 190 federally recognized tribal justice systems in the United States. The information to be collected will include, but not be limited to number of courts; number of facilities; codes and statutes; staffing; budgets; case processing procedures and policies; data entry systems; services offered by the courts; and other emerging criminal justice issues. It is also anticipated that there will be a need to institutionalize the statistical data collection process for regular collection cycles to as part of an ongoing BJS tribal data collection system.

Program Name Criminal History Record Information Sharing Project
Grantee Nlets
FY 2012 Funding $230,000
OJP Sponsor BJS
Web Link bjs.ojp.usdoj.gov
Program Contact Howard Snyder, (202) 616-8305, Howard.Snyder@usdoj.gov
Program Description
The current model for the Criminal History Record Information Sharing (CHRIS) database ignores the prosecution segment and only has a few general data fields from the supervision segment. This supplemental work would enhance the CHRIS layout to include multi-state prosecution and custody data and would help to expand or supplement the recidivism research, as well as other BJS national data collection projects. It would also enable BJS to extract samples of rap sheets to support additional recidivism and other BJS statistical efforts.

Appendix B

Formula Grants

Program Name State Formula and Block Grant Programs Training and Technical Assistance
Grantee American Institutes for Research
FY 2012 Funding $1,200,000
OJP Sponsor OJJDP
Web Link www.ojjdp.gov
Program Contact Elizabeth Wolfe, (202) 514-0582, Elizabeth.Wolfe@usdoj.gov
Program Description
OJJDP expects to continue to fund the American Institutes for Research (AIR) to provide training and technical assistance to national, state, and local-level grantees and non-grantees. OJJDP expects that this training and technical assistance will assist them in planning, establishing, operating, coordinating, and evaluating delinquency prevention and juvenile justice systems improvement projects. Additionally, AIR will coordinate OJJDP's state training conferences.

Program Name: Edward Byrne Memorial Justice Assistance Grant (JAG) Program
FY 2012 Funding $392,971,365
OJP Sponsor BJA
Web Link www.bja.gov/funding.aspx
Program Contact Darius LoCicero, (202) 514-2553, Darius.LoCicero@usdoj.gov
Program Description
The JAG program is the leading source of federal justice funding to state and local jurisdictions. JAG provides states, tribes, and local governments with critical funding necessary to support a range of program areas including law enforcement; prosecution and court; prevention and education; corrections and community corrections; drug treatment and enforcement; planning, evaluation, and technology improvement; and crime victim and witness initiatives. JAG funds may be used to address crime by providing services directly to individuals and communities; and by improving the effectiveness and efficiency of criminal justice systems, processes, and procedures. JAG awards are four years in length and are distributed up front instead of on a reimbursement basis, allowing recipients to earn interest on their awards and generate additional funding for successful initiatives and future projects. On average, more than 40 percent of annual JAG funding is allocated to law enforcement personnel, initiatives, and equipment including, but not limited to, multijurisdictional drug and gang task forces, police cruisers, and less than lethal devices. Remaining JAG funding is used to support a variety of programs and initiatives in the areas of courts, corrections, treatment, and justice information sharing.

Program Name: John R. Justice Student Loan Repayment Program
FY 2012 Funding $3,595,366
OJP Sponsor BJA
Web Link www.bja.gov/funding.aspx
Program Contact Kim Ball, (202) 307-2076, Kim.Ball@usdoj.gov
Program Description
The John R. Justice (JRJ) Grant Program provides loan repayment assistance for local, state, and federal public defenders and local and state prosecutors, who commit to continued employment as public defenders and prosecutors for at least three years. To administer this program, BJA will award funds to each of the 50 states, territories, and the District of Columbia to serve eligible recipients working within the state's or District's jurisdiction.

Program Name Victim Compensation
FY 2012 Funding See description below
OJP Sponsor OVC
Web Link www.ovc.gov/fund/welcome.html
Program Contact Toni Thomas, (202) 307-5983, Toni.Thomas@usdoj.gov

Program Description
All states, the District of Columbia, the U.S. Virgin Islands, and Puerto Rico have established compensation programs for crime victims. These programs reimburse victims for crime-related expenses such as medical costs, mental health counseling, funeral and burial costs, and lost wages.

Although each state compensation program is administered independently, most programs have similar eligibility requirements and offer comparable benefits. Maximum awards generally range from $10,000 to $25,000, though a number of states have higher and lower maximums. Compensation is paid only when other financial resources, such as private insurance and offender restitution, do not cover the loss. Some expenses are not covered by most compensation programs, including theft, damage, and property loss. State compensation programs are not required to compensate victims in terrorism cases.

To receive compensation, victims must comply with state statutes and rules, which generally require victims to cooperate with reasonable requests of law enforcement and submit a timely application to the compensation program. VOCA funds supplement state efforts to compensate crime victims. Each state compensation program receives an annual grant equal to 60 percent of what the program spends in state money annually. Applications for VOCA formula grants may be submitted online **only** by the state agency designated by the governor to administer the VOCA victim compensation and assistance program.

Program Name Victim Assistance
FY 2012 Funding See description below
OJP Sponsor OVC
Web Link www.ovc.gov/fund/welcome.html
Program Contact Toni Thomas, (202) 307-5983, Toni.Thomas@usdoj.gov
Program Description
States and territories receive VOCA funds to support community-based organizations that serve crime victims. More than 4,000 grants are made to domestic violence shelters, rape crisis centers, child abuse programs, and victim service units in law enforcement agencies, prosecutors' offices, hospitals, and social service agencies. These programs provide services that include crisis intervention, counseling, emergency shelter, criminal justice advocacy, and emergency transportation.

States and territories are required to give priority to programs serving victims of domestic violence, sexual assault, and child abuse. Additional funds must be set aside for underserved victims, such as survivors of homicide victims and victims of drunk drivers.

All states, the District of Columbia, the U.S. Virgin Islands, and Puerto Rico receive a base victim assistance amount of $500,000 each. The territories of the Northern Mariana Islands, Guam, and American Samoa each receive a base amount of $200,000. Additional funds are distributed based on population. Applications for VOCA formula grants may be submitted online **only** by the state agency designated by the governor to administer the VOCA victim compensation and assistance program.

Program Name Residential Substance Abuse Treatment for State Prisoners (RSAT) Formula Grant Program
FY 2012 Funding $8,688,415
OJP Sponsor BJA
Web Link www.bja.gov/funding.aspx
Program Contact Naydine Fulton-Jones, (202) 514-6661 Naydine.Fulton-Jones@usdoj.gov
Program Description
RSAT helps states and local governments to develop and implement substance abuse treatment programs in state and local correctional and detention facilities and to create and maintain community-based aftercare services for offenders. The goal of RSAT is to break the cycle of

drugs and violence by reducing the demand for, use, and trafficking of illegal drugs. RSAT enhances the capability of states and units of local government to provide residential substance abuse treatment for incarcerated inmates; prepares offenders for their reintegration into the communities from which they came by incorporating reentry planning activities into treatment programs; and assists offenders and their communities in the reentry process through the delivery of community-based treatment and other broad-based aftercare services.

RSAT funds may be used to implement three types of programs: residential, jail-based, and aftercare. Applications involving partnerships with community-based substance abuse treatment programs are given priority consideration. RSAT programs provide individual and group treatment activities for offenders and must last between 6 and 12 months; be provided in residential treatment facilities set apart from the general correctional population; focus on the substance abuse problems of the inmate; develop the inmate's cognitive, behavioral, social, vocational, and other skills to solve the substance abuse and related problems; and require urinalysis or other proven reliable forms of drug and alcohol testing of individuals assigned to RSAT programs in correctional facilities.

The Advocates for Human Potential (AHP) group currently serves as the RSAT training and technical assistance (TTA) providers, assisting grantees and sub grantees with all RSAT programming needs. AHP will be assisted by partners from TASC and the AdCare Criminal Justice Services to provide a comprehensive array of TTA needs including assisting corrections administrators and substance abuse directors in identifying and defining TTA needs; developing and testing trainer curriculum (including Web-based platforms); and developing cost-effective technical assistance responses, including telephonic, Web-based (podcasts and Webinars), in-person consultation, and publication development and dissemination.

Appendix C

Glossary

Acronyms:

AAG – Assistant Attorney General

AAMVA – American Association of Motor Vehicle Administrators

ABA – American Bar Association

APA – Association of Prosecuting Attorneys

APPA – American Probation and Parole Association

ASCA – Association of State Correctional Administrators

ATF – Bureau of Alcohol, Tobacco, Firearms and Explosives

AWA – Adam Walsh Child Protection and Safety Act of 2006

BIA – Bureau of Indian Affairs

BOP – Bureau of Prisons

BJA – Bureau of Justice Assistance

BJS – Bureau of Justice Statistics

CASA – Court Appointed Special Advocate

CASOM – Comprehensive Approaches to Sex Offender Management

CFR – Code of Federal Regulations

COPS – Office of Community Oriented Policing Services

CCTAP – Criminal Courts Technical Assistance Program

CISA – Criminal Information Sharing Alliance

DCPI – Adult Drug Court Planning Initiative

DHS – Department of Homeland Security

DOJ – Department of Justice

DOL – Department of Labor

DMI – Drug Market Intervention

DRP – The Data Resources Program

EUDL – Enforcing Underage Drinking Laws

GRF – Graduate Research Fellowship

HHS – Department of Health and Human Services

HSIN – Homeland Security Information Network

HUD – Department of Housing and Urban Development

IAA – Interagency Agreement

ICAC – Internet Crimes Against Children

JAG – (Edward Byrne Memorial) Justice Assistance Grant

JIS – Justice Information Sharing

JMHCP – Justice and Mental Health Collaboration Program

NACJD – National Archive of Criminal Justice Data

NASCIO – National Association of State Chief Information Officers

NBPI - Northern Border Prosecution Initiative

NCIRC – National Criminal Intelligence Resource Center

NCRP – National Corrections Reporting Program

NCSL – National Conference of State Legislatures

NCVS – National Crime Victimization Survey

NDCI – National Drug Court Institute

NICS – National Instant Criminal Background Check System

NIEM – National Information Exchange Model

NIJ – National Institute of Justice

NJC – National Judicial College

NMVTIS – National Motor Vehicle Title Information System

NPS – National Prisoner Statistics

NTTAC – National Training and Technical Assistance Center

OAAG – Office of the Assistant Attorney General

OJP – Office of Justice Programs

OJJDP – Office of Juvenile Justice and Delinquency Prevention

ONDCP – Office of National Drug Control Policy

OVC – Office for Victims of Crime

OVW – Office on Violence Against Women

PDMP – Prescription Drug Monitoring Program

RISS – Regional Information Sharing Systems

RSAT – Residential Substance Abuse Treatment

SAA – State Administering Agency

SANE – Sexual Assault Nurse Examiner

SAR – Suspicious Activity Reporting

SART – Sexual Assault Response Team

SAVIN – Statewide Automated Victim Information and Notification

SJS – State Justice Statistics Program

SMART – Office of Sex Offender Sentencing, Monitoring, Apprehending, Registering, and Tracking

SORNA – Sex Offender Registration and Notification Act

TTA – Training and Technical Assistance

USPIS – United States Postal Inspection Service

UCMN – Urban Court Managers Networks

VA – Veterans Administration

VOCA – Victims of Crime Act

Definitions:

Appropriation(s): The act of appropriating, setting apart, or assigning funding for a particular use; specifically, an act of a legislature authorizing money to be paid from the treasury for a special use.

Cold case: A crime or accident that has not been solved and is not the subject of current criminal investigation or civil litigation, but for which new information could emerge from new witness testimony, re-examined archives, or retained material evidence.

Competitive grant: A financial award for which a federal agency has the discretionary power to select the recipient from among all eligible recipients; decide to make or not make an award based on the programmatic, technical, or scientific content of an application; and determine the amount of funding to be awarded (also known as discretionary grants).

Consortium: An association of two or more individuals, companies, organizations, or governments (or any combination of these entities) with the objective of participating in a common activity or pooling their resources to achieve a common goal.

Co-occurring disorder: A co-occurring disorder, also called a dual diagnosis, occurs when an individual has both mental health and substance abuse treatment needs.

Criminal aliens: Both legal and illegal immigrants who have, on at least one occasion, become the object of the criminal justice system.

Discretionary grant: A grant awarded directly by OJP to eligible recipients. While discretionary grants are most often awarded on a competitive basis, some grants may be awarded on a noncompetitive basis, often based on congressional direction.

Earmark grant: A grant appropriated by Congress prior to a peer review. The term "earmark" is a reference to the *Congressional Record* where awards are written into legislation, specifically with grant applicants' names, activities, and dollar amounts.

Epidemiological: An epidemiological study is a population study designed to examine the scientific and medical study of the causes and transmission of disease within a population.

Evidence-based: Evidence-based practice refers to the use of research and scientific studies as a basis for determining the best practices in a field.

Forensic science (forensics): The application of a broad spectrum of sciences to answer questions of interest to a legal system, particularly in relation to a crime or civil action.

Formula or block grant: A grant awarded directly by OJP to an eligible recipient as authorized by statute. For formula and/or block grant programs, statutes or appropriations acts specify how the funds will be allocated among the eligible recipients, as well as the method by which an applicant must demonstrate its eligibility for that funding. Examples of this type of grant at OJP include the OJJDP Juvenile Accountability Block Grants Program and the OVC VOCA Victim Compensation Formula Grants. The award amount is calculated by a formula, and may vary among programs. Award calculations may consider such factors as population, census data, juvenile offender population, and Part 1 violent crimes reported to the FBI. Formula grant programs can be either for a specific purpose (e.g., assisting juvenile offenders) or related to public safety in general. The dollar amount available to applicants under each program is included in the solicitation. The specific recipient for state formula programs should be designated by each state. For state formula programs, OJP maintains a list of the designated agencies authorized by each state to administer these programs.

Fusion center: A terrorism prevention and response center. Fusion centers were established through a joint project between OJP and DHS between 2003 and 2007 and gather information not only from government sources but also from their partners in the private sector. They are designed to promote information sharing at the federal level among agencies such as the CIA, FBI, DOJ, U.S. military branches, and state and local governments.

Geospatial: A term to describe the combination of spatial software and analytical methods with terrestrial or geographic datasets.

Interagency Agreement (IAA): An agreement between two or more agencies.

Multidisciplinary: The involvement of two or more disciplines or professions in the provision of integrated and coordinated services, including evaluation and assessment activities.

National Information Exchange Model (NIEM): An XML-based information exchange framework from the United States. NIEM represents a collaborative partnership of agencies and organizations across all levels of government (federal, state, tribal, and local) and with private industry.

Noncompetitive grant: A grant that resembles a contract more than a grant. Noncompetitive grants are automatically awarded to institutions that qualify for legally defined formulas. Organizations agree to conduct activities in order to achieve a specific purpose based on an established program. The organization completes forms and assurances to secure funds.

One-stop location: Providing a comprehensive selection of goods or services at a single location.

Recidivism: Relapse into criminal behavior, often after receiving sanctions or undergoing intervention for a previous crime.

Roundtable: A meeting of peers for discussion and exchange of views.

State Administering Agency: An agency designated and authorized to administer state formula programs. Many OJP formula grants are awarded directly to state governments, which then set priorities and allocate funds within that state. For more information on how a state intends to distribute formula grant funds, contact the administering state agency.

Statistical Analysis Centers (SAC): SACs are state agencies that collect, analyze, and disseminate justice data. They contribute to effective state policies through statistical services, research, evaluation, and policy analysis.

Victims of Crime Act: This federal law, passed by Congress in 1984 and amended in 1988, called for the establishment of the Office for Victims of Crime and created the Crime Victims Fund, which provides non-appropriated funds to states for victim assistance and compensation programs that offer support and services to those affected by violent crimes.

Webinar: Short for *Web-based seminar*: a presentation, lecture, workshop, or seminar that is transmitted over the Internet. A key feature of a webinar is its interactive element—the ability to give, receive, and discuss information. A webinar is fundamentally different from a webcast, in which the data transmission is one way and does not allow interaction between the presenter and the audience.

Appendix D

Frequently Asked Questions about Applying for Grants Online

Q: How long does it take to register in Grants.gov or set up my account in the OJP Grants Management System (GMS)?

> **A: Grants.gov:** The registration process can take 1–3 weeks depending on your organization. Many factors contribute to this timeframe. See Get Registered on Grants.gov for details and instructions.
>
> **GMS:** About 3–5 days, but you should begin the application process as soon as possible, particularly if you are a first time user. For assistance with the electronic application process, call the GMS toll free hotline at 1-888-549-9901. The hotline is available from 7 a.m. to 9 p.m. eastern time, Monday through Friday.

Q: How do I access and get started with my online application?

> **A: Grants.gov:** Go to Search Grant Opportunities on Grants.gov.
>
> **GMS:** Go to Funding Opportunities at OJP. This site links users directly to GMS and the *GMS Application Procedures Handbook*, which gives step-by-step instructions. Click on the solicitation that interests you. Then select "Logon directly to the Grants Management System (GMS)," to apply for grant funding. If you have not previously used GMS, click on "New User? Register Here," and follow the onscreen instructions to register. After you register, select the name of the solicitation to which you are responding.

Q: What do I need to have ready before I apply online?

> **A: Grants.gov and GMS:** You will need a Dun and Bradstreet (D&B) Data Universal Numbering System (DUNS) number to register. Your application will not be considered complete until you provide a valid DUNS number.
>
> EXCEPTION: Individuals who would personally receive a grant or cooperative agreement from the federal government, apart from any business or nonprofit organization that they may operate, are not required to obtain a DUNS number. If this exception applies, enter any nine digits into the space provided. You can receive a DUNS number at no cost by calling the dedicated toll free DUNS number request line at 1-866-705-5711. If you have questions, contact OJP's Office of the Chief Financial Officer's Customer Service Center at 1-800-458-0786.
>
> Grants.gov has additional registration requirements. See Get Registered on Grants.gov for details.

Q: What types of files can I upload into Grants.gov and GMS?

> **A:** You must use one of these three formats to upload documents into Grants.gov and GMS: Portable Document Format (.pdf), Microsoft Word (.doc), or ascii (.txt).

Q: When will I know if my application is selected for funding?

> **A:** The application review process (including peer review, decision making, and other considerations) may take 6 months or longer. Notices of award and non-award are sent about 6 months after the closing date of a solicitation. Information regarding the status of awards is not available until notifications have been sent. Awards are posted regularly on the websites of OJP and its Bureaus.

Appendix E

2011 National Survey of Indigent Defense Services
2013 National Crime Victims' Rights Week (NCVRW) Community Awareness Project
2013 National Crime Victims' Rights Week (NCVRW) Resource Guide

A

Action Partnerships for Membership, Professional, and Community Service Organizations Responding to Poly-Victimization Issues
Adam Walsh Act (AWA) Implementation Grant Program
Adult Drug Court Planning Initiative (DCPI)
Adult Drug Court Technical Assistance Program
Adult Drug Court Training Initiative
American Indian and Alaska Nation Sexual Assault Nurse Examiner and Sexual Assault Response Team Program (AI/AN SANE-SART)
American Indian and Alaska Native Training and Technical Assistance (TTA) Program
Annual Survey of Jails
Annual Survey of Probation and Parole, 2011-2014
Anti-Human Trafficking Task Force Initiative Training and Technical Assistance
Applied Research and Development in Forensic Science for Criminal Justice Purposes
Arrest-Related Deaths Program, 2011-2014
Assessment and Collection of Administrative Data on Elder Abuse, Mistreatment, and Neglect

B

Basic Scientific Research to Support Forensic Science for Criminal Justice Purposes
BJS Data Resource Center Program
BJS Visiting Fellows
Building and Enhancing Criminal Justice Researcher-Practitioner Partnerships
Bulletproof Vest Partnership (BVP)
Byrne Criminal Justice Innovation Program

C

Capital Case Litigation Initiative (CCLI)
Capital Punishment, 2010-2012
Census of Law Enforcement Training Academies, 2012
Census of State and Local Law Enforcement Agencies
Census of Tribal Courts
Children's Advocacy Centers
Children's Justice Act Partnerships for Indian Communities Grant Program
CIO & State Coordination for Information Sharing and Technology Coordination
Community-Based Violence Prevention Field-Initiated Research and Evaluation Program
Community-Based Violence Prevention Program
Coordinated Tribal Assistance Solicitation
Court Appointed Special Advocate Programs

Crime Analysis Center Improvement Program
Criminal, Civil, and Regulatory Responses to White Collar Crime Program
Criminal History Record Information Sharing Project

D

Data Resources Program 2012 for the Analysis of Existing Data
Deaths in Custody Reporting Program, 2012-2015 Data Collection
Defending Childhood Task Force Recommendation Technical Assistance
Determining the Relationship between Stress and Unexplained In-Custody Deaths
Desistance from Crime Over the Life Course
DNA Backlog Reduction Program
Drug Court Discretionary Grant Program
Drug Market Intervention Initiative

E

Edward Byrne Memorial Competitive Grant Program - National Initiatives
Edward Byrne Memorial Justice Assistance Grant (JAG) Program
Enforcing Underage Drinking Laws (EUDL) Program
Enforcing Underage Drinking Laws Field-Initiated Research and Evaluation Program
Enhanced Collaborative Model to Combat Human Trafficking
Evaluability Assessment of Law Enforcement Agencies Using the Data-Driven Approaches to Crime and Traffic Safety
Evaluability Assessments of the Circles of Support and Accountability Model
Evaluating the Impact of the NIJ Body Armor Program
Evaluation of the FY 2011 Bureau of Justice Assistance Second Chance Act Adult Reentry Program for Planning and Demonstration Projects
Evaluation of the Implementation of the Sex Offender Treatment Intervention and Progress Scale
Evaluation of the Office of Juvenile Justice and Delinquency Prevention FY 2010 Second Chance Act Juvenile Offender Reentry Demonstration Projects

F

Family Drug Court Programs
Federated Identity, Privilege Management, and Technical Privacy Implementation
Federated Identity, Privilege Management, and Technical Privacy TTA Implementation
Field-Initiated Research and Evaluation Program
Firearm Inquiry Statistics Program

G

Global Support For National Policy, Practice, and Technology

H

Harold Rogers Prescription Drug Monitoring Program (PDMP)
Harold Rogers Prescription Drug Monitoring Training and Technical Assistance Program

I

Identifying Culturally Responsive Victim-Centered Restorative Justice (VCRJ) Strategies
Identity Theft Victim Assistance Networks
The Impact of Different Safety Equipment Modalities on Reducing Correctional Officer Injuries
Improving Correctional Agency Information Sharing
Internet Crimes Against Children Commercial Child Sexual Exploitation

J

John R. Justice Student Loan Repayment Program
Judicial Training
Justice and Mental Health Collaboration Program (JMHCP)
Justice and Mental Health Collaboration Program (JMHCP) State-Based Capacity Building Program (CBP)
Justice and Mental Health Collaboration Training and Technical Assistance Program
Justice Information Sharing Architecture and Implementation Support
Justice Information Sharing Training and Technology Assistance
Justice Reinvestment

K

L

Longitudinal Data on Teen Dating Violence: Post Doctoral Fellowship

M

Mentoring Research Best Practices Program
Methodological Research To Support the Redesign of the National Crime Victimization Survey (NCVS)
Missing Alzheimer's Program
Multi-Site Mentoring Enhancement Demonstration Project
Multi-State Mentoring Programs

N

National Crime Victimization Survey
National Criminal History Improvement Program (NCHIP)
National Corrections Reporting Program (NCRP)
National Drug Court Resource Center
National Field Generated Demonstration Projects Responding to Poly-Victimization Issues
National Field Generated Training, Technical Assistance and Demonstration Project
National Forum on Youth Violence Prevention Training and Technical Assistance
National Gang Center
National Information Exchange Model (NIEM) Program Support
National Instant Criminal Background Check System(NICS) Act Record Improvement Program (NARIP)
National Intertribal Youth Summit
National Juvenile Court Data Archive
National Juvenile Probation Census Project
National Mentoring Programs
National Pretrial Reporting Program

National Prisoner Statistics (NPS-1)
National Use of Force Data Collection Design
NCVS Victim/Offender Overlap and Victimization
NIJ Body Armor Challenge
NIJ Ph.D. Graduate Research Fellowship Program
Northern Border Prosecution Initiative (NBPI)

O

P

Paul Coverdell Forensic Science Improvement Grants Program
Postconviction DNA Testing Assistance Program
Post Secondary Education: Integrating Crime Victims' Issues into University and College Curricula
PREA Demonstration Projects to Establish "Zero Tolerance" Cultures for Sexual Assault Program (Prison Rape Prevention and Prosecution Program)
Protecting Public Health, Safety, and the Economy from Counterfeit Goods and Product Piracy: The Intellectual Property Theft Enforcement Program

Q

R

Reducing Electronic Crime
Replication Research on Sexual Violence Case Attrition
Research and Evaluation in Justice Systems
Research and Evaluation on Children Exposed to Violence
Research and Evaluation on Metropolitan Crime
Research and Evaluation on Trafficking in Persons
Research and Evaluation on Violence Against Women: Sexual Violence, Stalking, and Teen Dating Violence
Research on Domestic Radicalization
Research on Illegal Prescription Drug Market Interventions
Research on the Impact of Technology on Policing Strategies in the 21st Century
Research on the Link between Victimization and Offending
Research on Policing
Residential Substance Abuse Treatment for State Prisoners (RSAT) Formula Grant Program

S

Second Chance Act Adult and Juvenile Offender Reentry Demonstration Projects
Second Chance Act Adult and Juvenile Offender Reentry Demonstration Projects (Section 101)
Second Chance Act Co-Occurring Substance Abuse and Mental Health Disorders (Section 201)
Second Chance Act Demonstration Field Experiment: Fostering Desistance through Effective Supervision
Second Chance Act Family-Based Prisoner Substance Abuse Treatment Program (Section 113)
Second Chance Act Technology Careers Training Demonstration Projects for Incarcerated Adults and Juveniles (Section 115)
Second Chance Mentoring Program (Section 211)
Services for American Victims of Domestic Violence Overseas
Services for Victims of Human Trafficking
Services for Victims of Human Trafficking Fellowship Program
Seventh National SART Training Conference
Sexual Assault Forensic Medical Examination Telemedicine Center: An Innovative Pilot Project

SMART FY 2012 Maintenance and Operation of the Dru Sjodin National Sex Offender Public Website
SMART FY 2012 Professional Development Fellowship Program
Smart Probation: Reducing Prison Populations, Saving Money, and Creating Safer Communities
SMART Promoting Evidence Integration in Sex Offender Management: Circles of Support and Accountability for Project Sites
SMART Promoting Evidence Integration in Sex Offender Management: Circles of Support and Accountability Training and Technical Assistance Program
SMART Promoting Evidence Integration in Sex Offender Management: Implementing Sites of the Sex Offender Treatment
SMART Promoting Evidence Integration in Sex Offender Management: Sex Offender Treatment Intervention and Progress Scale Training and Technical Assistance Project
Social Science Research on Indigent Defense
Solving Cold Cases with DNA
Southwest Border Prosecution Initiative (SWBPI)
State Criminal Alien Assistance Program (SCAAP)
State Criminal Justice Technology Coordination and Enhancements Program
State Formula and Block Grant Programs Training and Technical Assistance
State Justice Statistics Program for State Statistical Analysis Centers
State Justice Statistics Technical Assistance Program
State Legislative Education and Action Project
State Victim Assistance Academy (SVAA) Continuation
State Victim Assistance Academy (SVAA) New
Statewide Adult Drug Court Technical Assistance Program
Supplementary Study of Victimization of People Residing in Group Quarters
Survey of Prison Inmates, 2012

T

Technical Assistance and Justice Policy Program
Testing Geospatial Police Strategies and Exploring Their Relationship to Criminological Theories
Training and Technical Assistance to Improve Understanding and Application of Research and Evaluation in Victim Services
Tribal Criminal and Civil Legal Assistance (TCCLA)
Tribal Justice Capacity Building Training and Technical Assistance Program
Tribal Youth Field-Initiated Research and Evaluation Program

U

U.S. Postal Inspection Service (USPIS) Public Awareness Campaign in Support of National Crime Victims' Rights Week
Using DNA Technology to Identify the Missing

V

VALOR
Victim Assistance
Victim Assistance and Compensation Professional Development Fellowship Program
Victim Assistance Professional Development Fellowship Program
Victim Assistance Professional Development Fellowship Program – Financial Fraud and Abuse Fellowship
Victim Compensation
Violent Gang and Gun Crime Reduction Program Project Safe Neighborhoods (PSN) Grant Program
Violent Victimization Among Racial and Ethnic Minorities

W

W.E.B. Du Bois Fellowship for Research in Race, Gender, Culture, and Crime
Wraparound Victim Legal Assistance Network Demonstration Project
Wrongful Conviction Review Program

X

Y

Z

www.ingramcontent.com/pod-product-compliance
Lightning Source LLC
Chambersburg PA
CBHW081842170526

45167CB00007B/2882